VEGGIE MEALS

VEGGIE MEALS

RACHAEL RAY'S
30-MINUTE MEALS

LAKE ISLE PRESS
New York

RACHAEL RAY'S 30-MINUTE MEALS
VEGGIE MEALS

Copyright © 2001 by Rachael Ray

Address all inquiries to:
Lake Isle Press, Inc.,
16 West 32nd Street, Suite 10-B
New York, NY 10001
e-mail: lakeislepress.com

Distributed to the trade by:
National Book Network, Inc.
4720 Boston Way
Lanham, MD 20706 Phone 1 800 462-6420
www.nbnbooks.com

Library of Congress Control Number: 2001131306
ISBN: 1-891105-06-x

Book design by Liz Trovato
Front cover photograph by Elizabeth Watt

First printing, April 2001
20 19 18 17 16 15 14 13 12 11

To farmers and fathers, who feed and care for us all

My grandpa Emmanuel kept a garden that fed his ten children, their friends, his friends, and many neighbors as well. More a necessity than a hobby, the garden meant food on the table.

Grandpa came from Sicily, settling into a landscape that seemed familiar, a small peninsula at Fort Ticonderoga in upstate New York, where many Italians, including my grandfather, found work as stone masons. His property on the shores of Lake George came with a sandy waterfront on one side, a steep hill protected from direct sunlight on its opposite face.

In the sandy soil he grew asparagus, strawberries, and raspberries. On the hillside, herb gardens bordered rows of salad greens, zucchini, eggplant, and green beans. Grandpa's grapes and dandelions fortified his wines; his homegrown escarole, garlic, onions, and potatoes, simmered or roasted to perfection, warmed many bellies on cool autumn nights.

Then there were the tomatoes, enough to can for the entire winter. In summer the children would eat the firm, red globes like apples, a salt shaker in hand, tomato juice dripping down their chubby chins. And at summer's end, green tomatoes fried in corn meal crusts were a special treat.

Cherry, pear, apple, and wild walnut trees dotted his distant fields. The fruits and nuts they bore were rewards for the children who finished chores, helped in the kitchen, or paid attention during Italian lessons.

Emmanuel Scuderi inspires me today. He was not rich or famous or Superman. He was something more: he loved the earth, the feeling of being outdoors; he loved to sing and laugh and play as much as his children did; all this after working 10- and 12-hour days setting heavy stones.

For me, a man of character builds deep, lasting relationships with his family and friends, just as a spiritual man cherishes his land. A great man is one who meets both of these challenges in a single lifetime. My grandfather was such a man.

ACKNOWLEDGMENTS

Every recipe I write is co-authored by a cast of thousands: family, friends, and friendly strangers from the many places my work takes me. Cooking is a collaborative effort. There are no new recipes, only variations on a theme. Years ago my mom came across a quotation that we remind one another of from time to time, usually after a satisfying meal: "The joys of the table belong equally to all countries and times."

I wish to give my love and special thanks to all the good cooks in my family: Mom, Manny, Maria, Pop, Nanny, and the cooks-in-training, Jessica and Nicholas. And to those of my close friends who share recipes and food with me, your generosity has not gone unnoticed; my love and appreciation to: Vicky, Bill, Alex, Renata, Sabia Rose, go-get-'em Ginny, sweet Anna Maria, terrific Tim, and dear Michael.

The televised version of The 30-Minute Meal is also a collaboration. Special thanks to WRGB News Channel 6, Schenectady, NY. WRGB is the world's first television station and without them, The 30-Minute Meal would be seen solely in my kitchen. Special thanks to to: SONY!!, Dave, Nate the Great, Leslie, Jim F., Al O., Bill, Bruce, Chris Conti, Tim, Tim and Tim, ED!!, Peter, Susan, Mike, Donna, Michelle-Nicole and Beau, Moya and Connie, Tom Long, and the many members of the technical staff that I have driven half-crazy with my less-than-adequate knowledge of "The Net" and all audiovisual equipment.

The live cooking demonstrations and community cooking classes of 30-Minute Meals are made possible by the Golub Corporation/Price Chopper. How can I ever thank all of you for the joy and opportunity to share food and fun with so many members of the community? The Golub Corporation is a misnomer; this is a family and I've been made to feel a part of it since day one. Special thanks to: Maureen (and thanks to JIMAPCO, for making sure I never get lost, unless I'm following Maureen...), Gail, Nancy, Cindy (that's Cindy Breslin, advertising), new mom Mel, Larry "We Know Meat!", Pat P., Dave "Now that's a big ad!," Mona G. G., Neil and Jane (such a nice couple!), and Louis. And more hugs and kisses to all my surrogate brothers and sisters in the stores — thanks!

The 30-Minute Meal books would not exist but for the work of talented editors, designers, and printers. Thank you. And where would I be in life without the support, guidance, and love of Elsa and Hiroko? (Too lost to know.) HUGE kisses and hugs to you both.

I thank God for a life blessed with more smiles than tears.

As always, I thank my dog Boo for eating my mistakes, and for always loving me, no matter what.

Contents

Introduction

If ever there was a time to consider "going veggie," this might be it. Given all the scary news about fast foods and beef, even serious meat and potato eaters are starting to ask for beans and greens, not just as a side salad or the occasional bundle of veggies, but as the main event, centerplate. This is a radical shift, let me tell you.

At my cooking classes and demonstrations, requests for meatless recipe ideas keep growing. Some people have given up red meat altogether, others have new vegetarians in the family, and new moms want ideas because "my kids won't eat vegetables." I say, try cookin' with vine-ripe tomatoes, earthy mushrooms, hearty beans, and fresh greens. With a great pasta, risotto, baked potato, or crusty bread, these veggies are awesome!

I'm convinced that food, to a large extent, is like a good joke: it's all in the delivery. For a delicious veggie meal, start with fresh, quality ingredients, vary the spices and textures, and present it wrapped, piled, or plated in a groovy arrangement. Season to taste, and use colors imaginatively, especially those wonderful fresh greens.

Most of all, have fun cooking. These veggie meals are quick and easy, of course, but more to the point, they are bursting with flavor, nutritious, and hugely satisfying.

RACHAEL RAY

Menus

Matchmaking is not my forte, except when it comes to foods. In menu-planning my matchmaking skills would put a single Jewish doctor's mother to shame!

While most recipes in this collection can stand alone as entrees, others are fun to mix and match.

Combine 2 or 3 of these 30-Minute Meals to make a carefree, vegetable menu for casual entertaining.

Bruschetta with Red Pepper and
Sun-Dried Tomato Spread
White Bean Salad
Green Gnocchi

Sesame Green Beans
Ginger and Scallion Couscous Salad
Eggplant Curry

Caesar Salad
Chick Pea and Cannellini Minestrone
Three Mushroom and Fontina-Stuffed Potatoes

Tabouleh Salad
Spicy Hummus and Crudite
Lentils with Pasta and Greens

Pumpkin Black Bean Soup
Quesadillas with Pico de Gallo and Guacamole

Zucchini Tomato Soup
Spinach Calzones

Portobello Burgers with Roasted Pepper Spread
Anti-Pasta Salad

Creamy Cauliflower Soup
Open-Faced Eggplant and Tomato Melts

Caprese Salad
Zucchini Risotto

Spinach Salad with Blue Cheese and Scallion
Polenta with Sun-Dried Tomato Sauce

Soups

Soups are ideal veggie meals. They are quick to make, nutritious, and always satisfying.

In this chaper, I've included some personal favorites, many with beans: escarole and cannellini bean, pumpkin and black bean, minestrone, chili for veg-heads, and more.

What, no tofu ? I must admit that in my kitchen, tofu is the one ingredient that got away. It's great in Asian dishes, but I prefer more robustly flavored ingredients, as you can see.

Campbell's is right, soup *is* good food, and I say, homemade is best!

Chili for "Veg-heads"

SERVES 4

Leftovers only get better.

2 tablespoons olive or vegetable oil (twice around the pan)

1 medium onion, chopped

1 medium bell pepper, red or green, seeded and chopped

1 jalapeno pepper, seeded and chopped

4 cloves garlic, minced

1 cup beer or vegetable broth

1 can (32 ounces) crushed tomatoes

1 can (14 ounces) black beans, drained and rinsed

1 can (14 ounces) red kidney beans, drained and rinsed

1 to 1 1/2 tablespoons ground cumin (half a palmful)

1 to 1 1/2 tablespoons ground chili powder (half a palmful)

6 dashes Red Hot or Tabasco sauce

Coarse salt, a few good pinches

1 cup spicy vegetarian refried beans

Shredded cheddar or chopped green onions, for garnish

Black bean, blue corn or flavored tortillas, for dipping

Heat oil in a deep pot over medium to medium-high heat. Add onion and peppers and sauté, stirring frequently, 3 to 4 minutes. Add garlic and cook one minute more. Add beer or broth and scrape up any good stuff from the bottom of the pan. Reduce the liquid by half, cooking it down for 2 or 3 minutes. Add tomatoes and beans and season with cumin, chili powder, Red Hot sauce, and salt. Thicken by stirring in refried beans.

Serve in bowls topped with shredded cheese or green onions with plenty of chips for dipping.

Red Beans and Rice Soup

SERVES 4

2 tablespoons vegetable or corn oil
   (twice around the pan)
1 medium onion, chopped
2 ribs celery from the heart of the stalk
1 medium green bell pepper, chopped
3 cloves garlic, crushed and minced
1 bay leaf, fresh or dried
1 1/2 teaspoons poultry seasoning, (1/3 palmful)
1 tablespoon ground cumin, (1/2 palmful)
Salt and pepper, to taste
2 ounces cayenne pepper sauce, such as Frank's
   Red Hot
1 can (15 ounces) red kidney beans, drained
   and rinsed
1 can (14 ounce) diced tomatoes, drained
1 quart (32 ounces) vegetable or chicken broth
1 1/2 cups enriched white rice

Heat oil in a deep pot over medium to medium-high heat. Add onion, celery, bell pepper, garlic, bay leaf, poultry seasoning, cumin, and salt and pepper to the pot. Sauté veggies, 5 minutes, stirring frequently. Add cayenne pepper sauce, red beans, tomatoes, and broth. Bring to a boil. Add rice, reduce heat, cover, and simmer 12 to 15 minutes, stirring occasionally, 'til rice is tender.

Three Bean Soup

SERVES 4

1 tablespoon canola or vegetable oil (1 turn
    around the pan)
1 medium onion, finely chopped
2 medium red-skinned potatoes, washed
    and diced
2 carrots, peeled and chopped
2 celery ribs from the heart of the stalk,
    chopped
1 bay leaf, fresh or dried
1 1/2 teaspoons ground cumin (1/2 palmful)
1 ounce cayenne pepper sauce, such as Red Hot
    or Tabasco (several drops)
1 can (15 ounces) red kidney beans, drained
    and rinsed
1 can (15 ounces) garbanzo beans (chickpeas),
    drained and rinsed
1 can (14 1/2 ounces) diced tomatoes in juice
1 tablespoon Worcestershire sauce (several drops)
3 cans (14 1/2 ounces each) vegetable or
    chicken broth
1/2 pound fresh green beans (a few handfuls)
    cut into thirds
A handful chopped fresh flat-leaf parsley

Heat a deep pot over medium to medium-high heat. Add oil, onion, potatoes, carrots, celery, bay leaf, cumin, and cayenne pepper sauce. Cover pot and cook veggies 5 minutes, stirring occasionally. Add beans, garbanzos, tomatoes, Worcestershire, and broth and bring to a boil. Add fresh green beans and simmer 3 to 5 minutes, 'til green beans are tender. Remove from heat and stir in fresh parsley. Remove bay leaf and serve.

Black Bean Soup

SERVES 4

1 tablespoon vegetable or canola oil (1 turn
　　around the pan)
1 large onion, finely chopped
3 cloves garlic, minced
2 jalapeño peppers, seeded and minced
1 bay leaf, fresh or dried
1 teaspoon ground coriander (1/3 palmful)
1 1/2 teaspoons cumin (1/2 palmful)
Coarse salt, to taste
2 cans black beans (15 ounces each), drained
　　and rinsed
1 can (14 1/2 ounces) vegetable or chicken broth
1 can (14 1/2 ounces) crushed tomatoes
4 scallions, sliced thinly on an angle
Tortilla chips, to garnish

SOUR CREAM SAUCE:
8 ounces sour cream or reduced-fat sour cream
1 to 2 ounces cayenne pepper sauce, such as
　　Tabasco or Red Hot
A handful fresh cilantro (about 2 tablespoons)

Heat oil in a deep pot over medium to medium-high heat. Add onion, garlic, jalapeños, and bay leaf. Season with coriander, cumin, and a little salt. Add beans, crushed tomatoes, and broth and bring to a boil. Reduce heat and simmer, 5 minutes. Serve in bowls topped with fresh scallions with tortilla chips on the side, for dipping.

For an extra garnish, combine sour cream, cayenne pepper sauce, and cilantro in a food processor and pulse-grind into a smooth sauce.

Pumpkin and Black Bean Soup

SERVES 4

1 tablespoon vegetable or canola oil (1 turn
   around the pan)

1 tablespoon butter (a couple pats)

1 medium onion, finely chopped

1 can (14 1/2 ounces) chicken or vegetable broth

1 can (14 1/2 ounces) diced tomatoes in juice

1 can (15 ounces) black beans, drained and rinsed

1 can (15 ounces) pumpkin puree

1/2 cup heavy cream (3 turns around the pan)

1 1/2 teaspoons curry powder (1/3 palmful)

1 teaspoon ground cumin, a little less than curry

3 pinches cayenne pepper (1/4 teaspoon)

Coarse salt, to taste

Heat a deep pot over medium heat. Add oil and butter. When butter melts, add onion and sauté, 5 minutes, 'til tender. Add broth, tomatoes, black beans, and pumpkin. Bring to a boil, reduce heat to low and stir in cream, curry powder, cumin, cayenne, and a few pinches salt. Simmer 5 minutes, adjust seasonings and serve.

Quick Red Cabbage Soup

SERVES 4

1 tablespoon vegetable or corn oil (1 turn around the pan)

1 medium onion, halved and very thinly sliced

2 Gala, Macintosh or Macoun apples, peeled and diced

2 jars (16 ounces each) red cabbage

1 tablespoon pickling spice (a palmful)

1 can (14 1/2 ounces) vegetable or chicken broth

1 can (14 1/2 ounces) crushed tomatoes

Coarse salt and black pepper, to taste

A few drops liquid smoke flavoring (optional)

Heat deep pot over medium to medium-high heat. Add oil, onion, and apples. Cover pot and cook 5 minutes, stirring occasionally. Add cabbage, pickling spice, broth, tomatoes, salt and pepper, and smoke flavoring. Bring to a boil, reduce heat and simmer, 10 minutes before serving.

Zucchini and Tomato Soup

SERVES 4

2 tablespoons extra-virgin olive oil (2 turns around the pan)

1 medium onion, finely chopped

3 cloves garlic, finely chopped

1 bay leaf, fresh or dried

1 medium zucchini, halved lengthwise, then sliced, 1/4-inch half-moons

1 jar roasted peppers (7 to 8 ounces), drained and diced

Salt and pepper, to taste

1 can (14 ounces) diced tomatoes in juice

1 can (32 ounces) crushed tomatoes or Italian tomato sauce

2 cans (14 ounces each) low-sodium vegetable broth

1 1/2 cups uncooked corkscrew pasta twists

A handful chopped fresh flat-leaf parsley

Grated Parmigiano Reggiano or Romano cheese, for the table

Heat a deep pot over medium heat. Add oil, onions, and garlic and sauté, 3 minutes, stirring frequently. Add bay leaf, zucchini, and roasted peppers; season with salt and pepper. Cover pot and cook, 5 minutes. Uncover, add diced and crushed tomatoes and broth. Increase heat to high and bring soup to a boil. Add pasta and return to a boil. Reduce heat, cover, and simmer 8 minutes, 'til pasta is cooked until al dente. Remove from heat and stir in parsley. Adjust salt and pepper, to taste. Remove bay leaf and serve in bowls topped with lots of grated cheese.

Quick Tomato and Basil Soup

SERVES 4

2 tablespoons extra-virgin olive oil (2 turns around the pan)

4 cloves fresh garlic, minced

1 medium onion, very finely chopped

2 cans (32 ounces plus 14 1/2 ounces) crushed tomatoes

1 can (14 1/2 ounces) vegetable broth

Coarse salt and black pepper, to taste

20 leaves fresh basil, torn or coarsely chopped

Garlic toast, for dipping

Heat a deep pot or skillet over medium-low heat. Add olive oil, garlic, and onion. Sauté onions 'til soft and sweet, 8 to 10 minutes. Add crushed tomatoes and broth. Season with salt and pepper, to taste. Bring to a boil, reduce heat, and simmer, 5 minutes longer. Remove from heat and stir in basil. Serve soup with lots of garlic toast for dipping.

Southwestern Corn and Pepper Pot

SERVES 4

2 tablespoons vegetable oil (2 turns around
the pan)
1 medium onion, chopped
3 cloves garlic, finely chopped
2 red bell peppers, seeded and chopped
1 teaspoon ground cumin (1/3 palmful)
1 cup chipotle salsa (available in Mexican
foods aisle)
1 can (32 ounces) stewed tomatoes
3 cups frozen corn kernels
2 cans (14 ounces each) vegetable broth
A handful fresh cilantro, finely chopped
(optional)
Coarse salt and black pepper, to taste
1 scallion, thinly sliced

Heat a deep pot over medium heat. Add vegetable oil, onion, garlic, and peppers, and sauté, 3 minutes. Sprinkle with cumin. Add salsa, tomatoes, corn, and broth. Bring soup to a boil, then reduce heat and simmer, 5 minutes. Stir in cilantro and season with salt and pepper, to your taste. Ladle into bowls and garnish with scallions.

Mashed Potato Soup
SERVES 4

MASHED POTATOES:

6 medium white potatoes, peeled and chunked

2 tablespoons butter

1/2 cup sour cream or reduced-fat sour cream

1/4 cup milk (2 splashes)

salt and pepper, to taste

SOUP:

4 cups prepared mashed potatoes (recipe
    above) or your own mix

1 cup heavy cream

2 cans (14 ounces each) vegetable broth

1/2 teaspoon cayenne pepper (a few pinches)

2 scallions, thinly sliced

1 cup sharp cheddar cheese, shredded

10 blades fresh chives, thinly sliced

In a large pot, cover potatoes with water and boil, 10 to 12 minutes, 'til tender. Drain potatoes and return to hot pot. Using a potato masher, combine potatoes with butter, sour cream, milk, and salt and pepper.

Heat a second pot over medium heat. Add prepared mashed potatoes. Whisk cream into potatoes until fully incorporated. Bring potatoes to a bubble and whisk in broth. Season with cayenne and stir in scallions. Simmer over low heat, 5 minutes. Remove from heat and serve in bowls topped with shredded cheddar and chives.

10-Minute Potato Leek Soup

SERVES 3

It's too easy!

1 leek, halved and very thinly sliced

3 cups reduced-fat or non-fat milk

2 cups water

1 brick (8 ounces) cream cheese or reduced-fat cream cheese, softened

3 3/4 ounces roasted garlic mashed potato flakes, such as Betty Crocker brand (1 pouch, each box contains 2 pouches)

A few grinds fresh black pepper, to taste

Rinse trimmed, thinly sliced leeks under cold water in a colander and drain very well. Bring milk, water, and leeks to a boil in a medium deep pot. Reduce heat to low and simmer, 5 minutes. Whisk in softened cream cheese until combined. Stir in potato flakes until soup becomes thick and smooth. Remove from heat, stir in pepper and serve.

Root Vegetable Chowder

SERVES 4

2 tablespoons butter

1 tablespoon vegetable oil (1 turn around the pan)

1 medium onion, chopped

1 medium parsnip, peeled and diced into
1/2-inch pieces

2 medium white-skinned potatoes, peeled and
diced into 1/2-inch pieces

1/2 pound baby carrots, cut into 1/2-inch slices

2 bay leaves, fresh or dried

1/2 teaspoon ground nutmeg, or a little freshly
grated whole nutmeg

1/2 teaspoon ground thyme (an even sprinkle
over the pot)

Coarse salt and pepper, to taste

2 tablespoons flour

2 cans (14 ounces each) vegetable broth

2 cups heavy cream or half-and-half

Heat a deep pot over medium heat. Melt butter into oil. Add onion, parsnip, potatoes, carrots, and bay leaves. Stir to coat vegetables and season with nutmeg, thyme, and salt and pepper. Sprinkle with flour and cook, 2 minutes. Whisk in broth. Bring soup to a boil, cover, and simmer, 15 minutes, 'til all veggies are tender. Uncover, stir in cream or half-and-half and heat through. Ladle into bowls and serve.

Escarole and White Bean Soup

SERVES 2

1 1/4 to 1 1/2 pounds escarole greens (1 head)

2 tablespoons extra-virgin olive oil (2 turns around the pan)

1 small boiling onion, chopped

4 large cloves garlic, chopped

A few pinches coarse Kosher salt

Freshly ground black pepper, to taste

1/2 teaspoon ground nutmeg or, a little freshly grated whole nutmeg

2 cans (14 1/2 ounces each) vegetable or chicken broth

1 can (15 ounces) cannellini beans, drained

Grated Parmigiano Reggiano or Romano cheese, for the table

Crusty bread, for mopping up

Trim away outer leaves of escarole and soak in cold water to wash. Drain greens very well in a colander, then on paper towels. Coarsely chop escarole and set aside.

Heat a deep skillet or pot over medium heat. Add oil, twice around the pan in a slow stream. Add onion and garlic and sauté, 2 to 3 minutes, stirring frequently. Add greens and allow them to wilt. Season with salt, pepper, and nutmeg, to taste. Add broth and beans and bring to a boil. Reduce heat and simmer, 5 minutes. Serve with grated cheese and bread.

Vegetable Soup
SERVES 4

2 tablespoons extra-virgin olive oil (2 turns around the pan)

1 medium onion, chopped

2 carrots, peeled and thinly sliced

2 ribs celery from the heart of the stalk, chopped

3 medium red-skinned potatoes, diced

1 bay leaf, fresh or dried

1 1/2 teaspoons Old Bay Seasoning (1/2 palmful)

1 can (14 1/2 ounces) red kidney beans, drained and rinsed

1 can (14 1/2 ounces) garbanzo beans, drained and rinsed

1 can (14 1/2 ounces) diced tomatoes in natural juice

Coarse salt and black pepper, to taste

3 cans (14 1/2 ounces each) vegetable or chicken broth

5 to 6 ounces spinach or baby spinach (1/2 sack fresh triple-washed) chopped or torn

Crusty bread, for the table

Heat a deep pot over medium to medium-high heat. Add oil, onion, carrots, celery, potatoes, bay leaf, and Old Bay seasoning. Cover pot and cook veggies, 5 to 8 minutes, stirring occasionally. Add beans, tomatoes and season with a little salt and pepper to taste. Add broth and bring to a boil. Simmer, 8 to 10 minutes longer. Remove from heat and stir in spinach. When spinach wilts, place in bowls and serve with crusty bread.

Chick Pea and Cannellini Minestrone
SERVES 6

2 tablespoons extra-virgin olive oil, (2 turns
	around the pan in a slow stream)
2 springs fresh rosemary, finely chopped, (about
	1 tablespoon)
1 medium onion, chopped
3 cloves garlic, minced
1 bay leaf, fresh or dried
1 can (14 ounces) chick peas (garbanzo beans),
	drained and rinsed
2 cans (14 ounces each) cannellini beans,
	drained and rinsed
1 medium carrot, peeled and finely chopped
2 ribs celery, from the heart of the stalk, chopped
1 can (14 ounces) diced tomatoes
8 cups vegetable broth (2 quart containers)
1 pound kale, trimmed and coarsely chopped
Coarse salt and pepper, to taste
1 cup ditalini pasta, uncooked
Grated Pamigiano Reggiano or Romano cheese,
	for the table
Warm, crusty bread

Heat a deep pot over medium heat. Add oil, rosemary, onion, garlic, and bay leaf, and sauté, 2 minutes. Add all of the beans, carrot, celery, tomatoes, broth, and kale. Season with salt and pepper and bring to a boil. Stir in raw pasta and return soup to boil. Cover, reduce heat, and cook, 10 minutes 'til veggies are tender and pasta is cooked to al dente. Remove soup from heat and adjust seasonings.

Ladle into bowls and serve with plenty of grated cheese, for topping and crusty bread, for mopping.

Gazpacho with Gusto

SERVES 2

Gazpacho travels well. Take a thermosful out for a day at the beach or add to a warm weather tailgate party.

1 can (32 ounces) crushed tomatoes

2 ounces cayenne pepper sauce, such as Tabasco or Frank's Red Hot

1/4 seedless, long European cucumber, peeled and cut into chunks

1/4 red onion, cut into chunks

1 serrano or jalapeno pepper, seeded

1/2 red bell pepper, seeded and cut into chunks

1 rib celery, from the tender heart of stalk, cut into chunks

A few sprigs fresh cilantro

Coarse salt and freshly ground black pepper, to taste

Wedges of fresh lime or lemon, for garnish

Combine all ingredients in a food processor and pulse grind until a thick, but smooth, soup is formed. Chill until ready to serve.

Serve in chilled glasses or bowls, garnished with wedges of fresh lime or lemon.

Creamy Cauliflower Soup

SERVES 4

SOUP:

1 medium head cauliflower

1 small cooking onion, finely chopped

1 quart reduced-fat or skim milk

2 cups water

1 tablespoon extra-virgin olive oil (1 turn around
   the pan)

1 tablespoon butter

Coarse salt and black pepper, to taste

1/2 cup herb or garlic-flavored instant
   potato flakes

GARNISH:

1 cup Italian bread crumbs

1 tablespoon extra-virgin olive oil

1/4 cup grated Parmigiano Reggiano or Romano
   cheese (a handful)

A handful chopped fresh flat-leaf parsley

Remove core of cauliflower and separate into small florets. Place florets, onion, milk, water, olive oil and butter in a deep pan or soup pot over medium-high heat. Bring to a boil. Season with a little salt and pepper. Cover with a tight-fitting lid, reduce heat to medium low, and cook, covered, 15 minutes, or until florets are very tender.

While cauliflower is simmering, toast bread crumbs in olive oil in a small pan over medium heat 'til deep golden. Remove pan from heat and stir in cheese and parsley.

To finish soup, remove cover and mash cauliflower, using a ricer or potato masher. Stir in potato flakes to thicken soup. Adjust seasonings. Ladle soup into bowls and top with toasted bread crumb mixture to serve.

Salads

Foods have their seasons. When it's cold outside, I want a big, deep bowl of minestrone. In summer, a cold plate of caprese, tomato and basil salad, ideal for nibbling, is irresistible

There are exceptions, however. In Spring, or at the beginning of Indian summer, a spinach salad is a nice start, but the cool night air makes me crave a little something extra, like bruschetta slathered with sun-dried tomato spread, a crispy, savory treat.

I come from a long line of big eaters who share this mantra: eat well and you can eat more. These versatile salad recipes will allow you to eat to your heart's content.

Grilled Vegetable Platter with Crumbled Ricotta Salata

SERVES 2 AS A SIMPLE SUPPER, 4 AS A FIRST COURSE OR SIDE DISH

2 red bell peppers

1 brown paper sack (medium size)

2 cloves garlic, peeled and cracked

Extra-virgin olive oil (about 1/3 cup)

2 stems fresh rosemary

2 medium baby eggplant, very thinly sliced lengthwise

2 small or 1 medium zucchini, halved, then thinly sliced lengthwise

A palmful fresh thyme leaves, stripped from stems and chopped (about 2 tablespoons)

Coarse salt and black pepper

5 or 6 ounces (1/3 pound) ricotta salata cheese, crumbled

Preheat broiler to high. Split red peppers down the center lengthwise and remove seeds and top. Place red peppers, skin side up, on a cookie sheet and place close to the hot broiler. Leave the door to the oven slightly ajar to allow any steam to escape as the peppers cook. Broil until the pepper skins are blackened. Place the charred peppers in a brown paper sack and close tightly; set aside.

Place garlic in a small dish and cover with olive oil (a couple of glugs). Rest the rosemary stems in the oil. Microwave on high for 30 seconds.

Heat a nonstick skillet or griddle pan to medium-high. Lightly baste sliced eggplant and zucchini with a touch of garlic oil using the rosemary as a pastry brush. Grill 2 minutes on each side in single layers, then arrange on a platter. Remove peppers from sack and peel charred skins away from flesh. Slice roasted peppers into strips and add to platter. Drizzle with any remaining garlic oil and sprinkle with chopped thyme, salt and pepper, and crumbled ricotta salata.

Asparagus Salad

SERVES 2 AS A SUPPER, 4 AS A SIDE DISH

1 pound thin asparagus, washed and dried

2 tablespoons soy sauce

1 tablespoon rice wine or white vinegar (a splash)

1 inch fresh gingerroot, grated

2 tablespoons dark brown sugar

2 tablespoons vegetable or canola oil (2 turns around the pan)

Zest of 1 orange

1 tablespoon sesame seeds (1/2 palmful)

6 ounces mixed mesculin greens

1/2 cup mandarin orange sections, drained or 1 navel orange, peeled and chopped

1/2 small red onion, finely chopped

Break asparagus spears with a gentle snap to free tender tops from tough part of the stalks. Steam in 1/4-inch simmering water, covered, 3 to 5 minutes. Rinse under cold water and drain.

Heat a nonstick skillet over medium to medium-high heat. Add soy sauce, rice or white vinegar, fresh ginger, sugar, and oil. Heat to a bubble. Add asparagus and coat with dressing. Sprinkle with orange zest and sesame seeds. Serve warm on a bed of mixed mesculin salad greens. Garnish with mandarin sections or diced navel orange and red onion.

White Bean Salad

SERVES 4 AS A SIDE DISH

2 cans (15 ounces each) cannellini beans, drained
and rinsed

2 cloves garlic, minced

2 tablespoons extra-virgin olive oil (2 turns
around the bowl)

4 sprigs fresh thyme, leaves stripped and
chopped (about 1 1/2 tablespoons)

6 sprigs fresh mint, finely chopped
(2 tablespoons)

Coarse salt and black pepper, to taste

Combine all ingredients in a large bowl and serve.

Lentil Salad

SERVES 2 AS A SUPPER WITH WARM PITA BREAD, 4 AS A SIDE DISH

1/2 pound lentils, green or other variety

1 bay leaf, fresh or dried

1 large plum tomato, seeded and diced

2 handfuls chopped fresh flat-leaf parsley
(about 1/4 cup)

2 to 3 tablespoons extra-virgin olive oil (2 glugs)

Juice of 1/2 lemon

A splash red wine vinegar

1 clove garlic, minced

1/2 teaspoon ground cumin (4 good pinches)

1/4 teaspoon allspice (2 pinches)

1/4 teaspoon ground coriander (2 pinches)

1/2 teaspoon paprika (4 pinches)

Coarse salt and black pepper, to taste

3 tablespoons prepared tahini sauce (optional)
or 2 tablespoons sesame tahini paste,
thinned with a splash of water (optional)

In a medium pot, cover lentils with water, add bay leaf, and bring to a boil. Reduce heat to simmer and cook until tender, about 20 minutes. Rinse under cold water and drain.

Combine lentils with tomato and parsley. Whisk the oil, lemon juice, vinegar, garlic, cumin, allspice, coriander, and paprika together. Pour dressing over lentils and coat evenly. Season with salt and pepper to taste. Top with a drizzle of tahini sauce.

Tabouleh Salad

SERVES 2 AS A MAIN COURSE, 4 AS A SIDE DISH

1 package (7 ounces) tabouleh salad mix, such as Near East or Fantastic Food brands

1 cup warm water

2 cloves garlic, minced

2 tablespoons extra-virgin olive oil (2 turns around the bowl)

1/4 seedless European cucumber or 1 pickling Kirby cucumber, peeled and chopped

1 vine-ripe tomato, seeded and diced

1/2 cup chopped fresh flat-leaf parsley (2 handfuls)

1/4 cup fresh mint leaves, finely chopped (8 sprigs)

Juice of 1 lemon

1/2 cup prepared tahini sauce

Warm pita bread

Combine seasoning packet and cracked bulgur in a bowl with 1 cup warm water, chopped garlic, and olive oil. Cover and refrigerate for 30 minutes.

While bulgur absorbs liquid, prepare the cucumber, tomato, and herbs.

To serve, combine prepared bulgur with cucumber, tomato, parsley, mint, and lemon juice. Drizzle with tahini sauce and serve with warm pita bread.

Tomato Basil Panzanella

SERVES 2 AS A SUPPER, 4 AS A STARTER

3 medium vine-ripe tomatoes, diced

20 leaves fresh basil, stacked, rolled into logs, then thinly sliced

1/2 pound fresh mozzarella, cubed into bite-size pieces (optional)

2 crusty, chewy rolls, cubed (day-old Italian is fine)

3 tablespoons extra-virgin olive oil (3 turns around the bowl)

1 1/2 tablespoons red wine vinegar (a couple splashes)

Coarse salt and black pepper, to taste

Combine all ingredients in a large bowl. Let stand for 10 minutes to allow bread to absorb juices, then serve.

Anti-Pasta Salad
with Bagna Cauda Dressing

SERVES 4

Bagna cauda is a warm dip of anchovies, garlic, and oil, often served with raw vegetables. We've lightened the taste, adding fresh lemon juice, and made anchovies optional for strict vegetarians.

1/2 pound thin asparagus spears, trimmed and washed

1/2 pound penne rigate, cooked until al dente

1 can (14 ounces) artichoke hearts in water, drained and coarsely chopped

1 large red bell pepper, roasted, peeled and diced or 1 jar (7 ounces) roasted red peppers, drained and diced

1 cup giardiniera Italian hot pickled vegetable salad, drained and chopped (found jarred in the Italian foods section of market)

8 ounces fresh mozzarella, diced

20 olives, mixed Sicilian green or oil-cured black, pitted and chopped

2 tablespoons capers, drained and chopped

DRESSING

1/3 cup extra-virgin olive oil (3 glugs)

1/2 teaspoon crushed red pepper flakes

4 cloves garlic, minced

2 tablespoons anchovy paste (optional)

A handful fresh flat-leaf parsley, finely chopped

Juice of 1 lemon

Black pepper, to taste

Cook asparagus in 1/2-inch boiling water for 3 minutes, covered. Cold shock the spears in a colander under running water and drain well. Cut into bite-size lengths.

In a large bowl, combine penne, asparagus, artichoke hearts, roasted peppers, giardiniera pickled vegetables, fresh mozzarella, olives, and capers.

In a small skillet over low heat, combine olive oil, crushed red pepper flakes, garlic, and anchovy paste. Sauté garlic until anchovy paste melts into the dressing and garlic sizzles in the oil. Remove from heat and stir in parsley and lemon juice. Pour dressing over salad, toss to coat, and season with black pepper, to taste.

Garden Panzanella

SERVES 2 AS A SUPPER, 4 AS A SIDE DISH

1 cubanelle pepper (light green Italian sweet),
    seeded and diced

1 small red bell pepper, seeded and diced

2 medium vine-ripe tomatoes, diced

1 pickling (Kirby) cucumber, peeled and chopped

8 ounces fresh mozzarella, cubed (optional)

1/2 small red onion, chopped

1 1/2 ounces capers (a handful), drained
    and rinsed

20 Kalamata olives, pitted, and coarsely
    chopped (See Note)

A handful chopped fresh flat-leaf parsley

20 leaves fresh basil, stacked, rolled into logs,
    then thinly sliced

3 crusty, chewy, stale rolls, cubed or 1/2 loaf
    stale Italian bread, cubed

1/3 cup extra-virgin olive oil (3 or 4 glugs)

3 anchovy fillets

3 cloves garlic, minced

2 tablespoons red wine vinegar (3 splashes)

Coarse salt and black pepper, to taste

2 ounces pignoli (pine) nuts, toasted in small
    pan or toaster oven 'til golden, to garnish

Combine veggies, parsley, basil, and bread in a bowl.

Place oil in a small bowl with anchovies and garlic. Microwave on high, 1 minute. Let stand, 5 minutes. Mash anchovies with a fork in the oil until they break up. Mix oil and vinegar. Pour evenly over salad and toss well. Season with salt and pepper. Let stand 10 to 15 minutes minimum, then serve, using pine nuts to garnish.

Note: Olives can be pitted by centering the flat of a wide knife blade over the olive and giving the blade a whack with the heel of your hand.

Greek Vegetable Salad-Stuffed Pitas

SERVES 2 AS A SUPPER, 4 AS A SIDE DISH OR STARTER

1 can (14 ounces) quartered artichoke hearts in
    water, drained

1/4 small red onion, thinly sliced

2 vine-ripe tomatoes, seeded and diced

1 small pickling (Kirby) cucumber or 1/4 seedless
    European cucumber, washed, peeled,
    and chunked

20 Kalamata olives, pitted and chopped
    (See Note, page 44)

1/2 cup chopped fresh flat-leaf parsley
    (2 handfuls)

8 ounces feta cheese, crumbled

Juice of 1 lemon

A generous drizzle extra-virgin olive oil

Coarse salt and black pepper, to taste

1 cup plain yogurt

1 clove garlic, finely chopped

2 tablespoons fresh dill, chopped

A pinch coarse salt and black pepper, to taste

4 large pitas, warmed

4 leaves romaine lettuce, from the heart

Combine first 9 ingredients in a bowl. Season with a little salt and pepper.

In a small bowl combine yogurt with garlic, dill, and salt and pepper. Line a warm pita with a lettuce leaf, fill with salad, and top with yogurt sauce.

Baby Spinach Salad with Pears and Walnuts

SERVES 2 AS A SUPPER, 4 TO 6 AS A STARTER

1 sack (10 ounces) washed baby spinach

1/4 medium red onion, thinly sliced

1 ripe Bosc pear, quartered, seeded, and
    thinly sliced

Juice of 1/4 lemon

6 ounces Asiago cheese, thinly sliced

2 ounces walnut meats (2 handfuls)

1/4 cup extra-virgin olive oil (3 glugs)

1 small shallot, very finely chopped

1 1/2 tablespoons white balsamic, pear-infused
    balsamic or white wine vinegar

A pinch sugar

Coarse salt and black pepper, to taste

Place spinach greens in a large shallow bowl. Scatter the greens with onion, pear (coated with lemon juice to retard browning), Asiago cheese, and walnut meats.

Pour olive oil into a small bowl. Add shallots and microwave for 1 minute on high. Let stand, 5 minutes. Whisk vinegar and a pinch of sugar into the oil. Drizzle dressing evenly over salad. Season with salt and pepper, toss, and serve.

Spinach Salad with Blue Cheese and Scallion

SERVES 2 AS A SUPPER, 4 AS A STARTER

1 sack (10 ounces) triple-washed spinach,
   stems removed

1/2 pound green beans, trimmed and halved

2 ounces pecan halves (a couple handfuls)

6 ounces blue cheese (dry, not creamy), crumbled

4 scallions, thinly sliced on an angle

1/4 cup extra-virgin olive oil (3 glugs)

1 1/2 tablespoons white wine vinegar

1/2 teaspoon Dijon mustard (a dab)

2 sprigs fresh tarragon, leaves stripped and
   finely chopped (about 1 tablespoon)

Coarse salt and black pepper, to taste

Place spinach in a large shallow bowl. Steam green beans for 5 minutes in a cup of simmering water, covered. Drain beans and cool by running under cold water. Scatter beans over greens. Sprinkle salad with pecans, blue cheese crumbles, and scallions.

Combine oil, vinegar, Dijon mustard, and tarragon with a whisk. Drizzle dressing evenly over salad, season with salt and pepper, toss, and serve.

Beet, Onion, and Orange Salad

SERVES 4

2 cans (15 ounces each) sliced beets, drained

1/2 medium red onion, peeled and thinly sliced

2 navel oranges, sectioned, peeled and diced

2 tablespoons extra-virgin olive oil

1 tablespoon red wine vinegar (a splash)

2 pinches sugar

A handful fresh flat-leaf parsley, finely chopped
    (2 to 3 tablespoons)

2 sprigs fresh oregano, finely chopped
    (1 tablespoon)

A few pinches coarse salt

Arrange beets and onion on a serving plate. Scatter plate with oranges. Using a fork, combine remaining ingredients in a small bowl. Pour dressing evenly over serving dish in a slow stream.

Orzo and Zucchini Salad

SERVES 4

3 tablespoons extra-virgin olive oil (3 turns around the pan))
1 medium zucchini, chopped into a small dice
4 cloves garlic, minced
1/2 pound orzo pasta, cooked until al dente, rinsed under cool water, and drained well
Juice of 1/2 lemon
1/2 cup fresh mint leaves, finely chopped (about 6 sprigs)
1/2 cup fresh flat-leaf parsley, finely chopped (a couple handfuls)
Coarse salt and pepper, to taste
Mixed baby greens, (optional)

Heat a medium skillet over medium heat. Add olive oil, zucchini, and garlic. Sauté zucchini, 5 or 6 minutes and remove from heat.

Place drained, cooked orzo in a bowl. Combine with zucchini and garlic, lemon juice, mint, and parsley. Toss and season with salt and black pepper, to taste. Serve on its own or on a bed of baby greens.

Couscous Salad
With Scallions and Ginger
SERVES 4

2 cups vegetable broth

2 tablespoons extra-virgin olive oil (2 turns
    around the pan)

1 inch fresh gingerroot, grated

3 tablespoons dried currants (a handful)

1 teaspoon curry powder (1/3 palmful)

1/2 teaspoon ground coriander

1/4 teaspoon allspice (a few pinches)

1/2 teaspoon coarse salt

1 package (5 ounces) plain couscous

1 navel orange, peeled, sectioned, and diced

3 scallions, thinly sliced on an angle

2 ounces slivered almonds

Combine first 8 ingredients in a small pot and bring to a boil. Reduce heat and simmer, 2 to 3 minutes, to steep the ingredient flavors into the broth. Remove from heat and stir in couscous. Cover pot and let stand 5 minutes. Fluff couscous with a fork. Stir in remaining ingredients. Serve warm or chilled on a bed of greens tossed with a light vinaigrette.

Caprese Salad

SERVES 2 AS A SIMPLE COLD SALAD SUPPER OR 4 AS A FIRST COURSE OR SIDE DISH

1 pound fresh mozzarella or fresh smoked
   mozzarella
2 large or 3 medium, firm vine-ripened tomatoes
20 leaves fresh basil
Extra-virgin olive oil, for drizzling
Coarse salt and cracked black pepper, to taste

Slice mozzarella and tomatoes into 1/4-inch thick slices. Alternating tomatoes, basil leaves and mozzarella arrange in a circular pattern on a serving platter. Drizzle with olive oil and season with salt and pepper, to taste.

Author's Note: Caprese and Caesar salads are known the world over. Though recipes for their preparation appeared in my original *30-Minute Meals* book, they are being reprinted here in a slightly revised version because I could not imagine a vegetarian cookbook without them.

Caesar Salad

SERVES 2 AS A MEAL

4 cloves garlic

Extra-virgin olive oil (about 1/3 cup total)

1 cup, packed, cubed, semolina bread
(day-old is fine)

Coarse black pepper, to taste

2 tablespoons anchovy paste (optional for
strict vegetarians)

1 teaspoon Worcestershire sauce (6 to 8 drops)

1 large egg yolk or 1/4 cup pasteurized
egg product

Juice of 1 large ripe lemon

2 hearts romaine lettuce, coarsely chopped

A little coarse salt, to taste

2 handfuls freshly grated Parmigiano
Reggiano cheese

Crack the garlic away from its skin with a good whack of your hand against the flat of your knife, centered on top of each clove. Rub the inside of your salad bowl with 1 clove of cracked garlic. Place that clove and a second clove aside. Mince the remaining 2 cloves and place in a small bowl.

Heat a small skillet over medium heat. Add 2 tablespoons olive oil (2 turns around the pan), and the 2 cracked cloves of garlic. When the garlic speaks by sizzling in oil, add bread and toast until golden, tossing occasionally, 6 to 8 minutes. Sprinkle cubed bread with a little pepper and remove from heat.

Combine chopped garlic and 3 glugs of olive oil (about 1/4 cup) in a small bowl or in a small skillet. Heat garlic and olive oil, either in a microwave oven for 1 minute, or over low heat on a stove top, 2 to 3 minutes. Stir anchovy paste into the warm olive oil with a fork and let stand until oil returns to room temperature.

Add Worcestershire sauce and egg yolk or egg product to salad bowl and stir with a fork. Add lemon juice and stir into egg. Add the olive oil, garlic, and anchovy mixture in a slow stream and continue to beat with a fork. Add romaine to bowl and toss to coat. Add a generous amount of cheese and croutons and toss again to coat. Season with salt and pepper, to taste.

Macaroni Salad with Tarragon Dressing

8 GENEROUS SIDE SERVINGS

A great salad to accompany a sandwich of ripe brie, lettuce, and tomato on a crusty baguette.
Perfect picnic food for the park or a blanket in your living room!

$1/2$ cup reduced-fat mayonnaise (4 rounded
    teaspoons)

2 tablespoons extra-virgin olive oil (2 glugs)

2 tablespoons white wine or tarragon vinegar
    (2 splashes)

2 tablespoons fresh tarragon (3 or 4 sprigs),
    chopped

1 pound elbow macaroni, cooked until al dente,
    drained and cooled

1 medium red bell pepper, seeded and
    finely diced

4 scallions, thinly sliced

1 cup frozen green peas, defrosted

Coarse salt and black pepper, to taste

Using a fork, combine mayonnaise, olive oil, vinegar, and tarragon together in a small bowl, whisking until smooth.

In a large bowl, combine macaroni, bell pepper, scallions, and peas. Spoon dressing over macaroni and veggies, and toss to coat evenly. Season with salt and pepper, to taste.

Risotto, Pasta, and Mediterranean-Style Entrees

I eat just about everything, including meat, but I could just as easily "go vegetarian" without difficulty. It must be my Mediterranean genes.

Many favorite family recipes are meat-free, well, sort of. My mamma's recipes for risottos, minestrone, and vegetable barley are meatless, but tell mamma to prepare any of these dishes without chicken or beef stock and she'll say, "pick something else to make for dinner!"

If you are a vegetarian, use vegetable broth and portobello stock as flavorful substitutes. Or, do it mamma's way. Your cooperation in helping me keep the family peace is greatly appreciated.

My Mamma's Risotto

SERVES 4 AS A SIMPLE SUPPER, 8 AS A SIDE DISH

6 cups vegetable broth (Mamma prefers chicken broth)

3 tablespoons butter

1 tablespoon extra-virgin olive oil (once around the pan)

1 small cooking onion, chopped

2 cups arborio rice

1/2 cup dry white wine

1/2 cup grated Parmigiano Reggiano or Romano cheese (a couple handfuls)

Coarse salt and black pepper, to taste

Place vegetable or chicken broth in a medium sauce pan. Bring to a slow boil, reduce heat to lowest setting, and let simmer.

In a deep sauce pan or skillet, melt butter into olive oil over medium heat. Add onion and sauté, 3 to 5 minutes until tender. Add rice and sauté, 2 minutes more. Add the wine (a couple of glugs) and let evaporate for 2 minutes. Add 1 cup of broth and let it get absorbed by the rice. Keep adding half of the broth remaining to the pan, stirring frequently until absorbed. Taste rice after 15 to 17 minutes and only add as much broth as needed to cook the rice al dente—tender, but with a little bite left to it. Remove from heat and stir in cheese. Season with salt and pepper, to taste, and serve.

Artichoke Risotto

Drain 1 can (15 ounces) of artichoke hearts packed in water and coarsely chop. Heat 2 tablespoons extra-virgin olive oil in a medium pan. Add 2 cloves minced garlic and sauté artichoke hearts, 2 or 3 minutes. Strip the leaves off a few stems of fresh thyme and chop, about 1 tablespoon. Stir the artichokes and thyme into the original recipe at the point when cheese is added.

Asparagus Risotto

Steam 1 cup of asparagus tips in 1/2 cup water. Drain and sauté tips in 2 tablespoons extra-virgin olive oil with 2 cloves minced garlic. Stir asparagus into the original recipe at the point when cheese is added.

Zucchini Risotto

Shred 2 small zucchini with a grater. Heat 2 tablespoons extra-virgin olive oil in a skillet over medium heat. Add 3 cloves of minced garlic. When garlic speaks by sizzling in oil, add zucchini. Sauté for 5 minutes and remove from heat. Add 2 tablespoons of fresh mint, chopped fine. Season with salt, to taste. Stir zucchini into risotto recipe at the point when cheese is added.

Porcini Risotto

SERVES 4 AS AN ENTRÉE, 8 AS A FIRST COURSE

1 ounce (two 1/2-ounce packets) dried porcini
    mushrooms
2 cups spring or filtered water
4 cups portobello stock (recipe follows), or
    beef broth
2 tablespoons extra-virgin olive oil (twice
    around the pan)
1 tablespoon butter (a pat)
2 shallots, finely chopped
1 1/2 cups arborio rice
1/2 cup cognac, or sherry
Coarse salt and black pepper, to taste
1 tablespoon fresh thyme (a few sprigs stripped
    from stems and chopped)
1/2 cup grated Parmigiano Reggiano cheese
    (a couple handfuls)

Place mushrooms in a small sauce pan and cover with 2 cups of water. Bring to a slow boil, reduce heat to lowest setting and simmer, 10 to 15 minutes, or until tender.

Place stock or broth in a second small pan over medium heat to warm.

In a deep skillet, heat olive oil and butter over medium to medium-high heat. Add shallots and sauté, 2 minutes. Add rice and sauté, 2 or 3 minutes more. Add cognac or sherry and allow the alcohol to burn off by reducing the liquid a minute more. Add half the stock or broth and reduce heat slightly to medium or medium low. Simmer, stirring frequently, 6 or 7 minutes.

Remove mushrooms from their liquid and reserve the cooking liquid. Coarsely chop the mushrooms and add them to the rice. Add mushroom liquid to the remaining stock or broth. Add half of total liquids remaining to the rice. Season with salt, pepper, and thyme.

Continue to cook the rice, stirring frequently, until the rice is tender, yet still creamy, adding the last of the liquids if necessary to achieve a texture pleasing to you. Stir in a few handfuls of freshly grated cheese and serve immediately. *Buon appetito!*

Portobello Stock
MAKES 4 CUPS

2 medium portobello mushroom caps
1 tablespoon extra-virgin olive oil (1 turn around
    the pan)
A few pinches coarse salt
1 boiling onion, quartered
1 bay leaf, fresh or dried
2 cans (14 ounces each) low-sodium vegetable
    broth

Thinly slice mushroom caps.

Heat a small deep pot over medium-high heat. Add olive oil and mushrooms and sprinkle with salt to draw juices out. Sauté 'til mushrooms begin to soften. Add onion and bay leaf. Reduce heat to medium low and cover. Cook 5 minutes, 'til mushrooms are dark and juicy. Add broth and simmer, 10 minutes longer. Strain and store broth in plastic tubs. Stock will keep up to 10 days in the fridge, 2 months in the freezer.

Pasta alla Trapanese: Pasta with Fresh Tomato Basil Sauce

SERVES 4

1/4 cup extra-virgin olive oil (4 turns around the pan)

4 large cloves garlic, finely chopped

3 scallions, sliced very thinly on an angle

6 vine ripe tomatoes, diced

Coarse salt and black pepper, to taste

1 pound fresh pasta — your choice, such as penne rigate or fusilli

20 leaves fresh basil, roughly cut or torn

Heat olive oil in a deep skillet over medium heat. Add garlic and gently sauté, until garlic speaks by sizzling in oil. Add scallions and sauté, 2 or 3 minutes more. Add tomatoes and season with salt and pepper, to taste. Reduce heat to medium low and simmer.

Bring salted water to a boil and cook fresh pasta until al dente. Drain well.

Stir basil into sauce. Bring heat back up to medium. Add pasta to sauce pan and toss until all ingredients are combined and hot.

Serve immediately with a green salad or Italian chunked vegetable salad and crusty bread.

Variation:

Add bits of fresh mozzarella to the dish when the pasta is being tossed with sauce.

Pestos

EACH RECIPE WILL PROVIDE ENOUGH SAUCE FOR 1 POUND OF PASTA

Pesto freezes beautifully. Store partial or whole batches in small plastic containers. Defrost several hours ahead of serving at room temperature. Never heat pestos; they will turn dark and bitter.

Spinach Pesto
MAKES 1 1/2 CUPS

2 cloves garlic, cracked away from skin

1/4 cup extra-virgin olive oil (a couple of glugs)

6 ounces baby spinach leaves (pre-washed packages in produce department)

1/2 cup grated Parmigiano Reggiano cheese (3 handfuls)

3 or 4 pinches ground nutmeg (1/2 teaspoon)

3 ounces walnuts, toasted in small sauce pan or toaster oven 'til golden

Coarse salt and black pepper, to taste

Place garlic in a small dish. Cover garlic with oil and microwave on high, 1 minute. Remove from microwave and let stand 5 minutes to cool.

Combine garlic and oil in a food processor with all remaining ingredients and pulse grind into a smooth paste. Toss with hot pasta cooked until al dente.

Parsley Pesto

Follow the recipe for Spinach Pesto, substituting 2 cups packed fresh flat-leaf parsley tops for the spinach and omitting the nutmeg.

Pesto Genovese

3 cups basil leaves (the yield of 1 large bunch)
2 cloves garlic, cracked away from skin
2/3 cup extra-virgin olive oil, divided in half
3 ounces pine nuts (a handful), lightly toasted
    in a small pan or in toaster oven
1/2 cup grated Parmigiano Reggiano cheese
    (3 handfuls)
Coarse salt, to taste

Place basil in a food processor. Place garlic in a small dish, cover with half the olive oil, and microwave on high, 1 minute. Remove from microwave and let stand 5 minutes to cool. Add garlic and oil and pine nuts to the processor and pulse grind into paste. Transfer to a bowl and slowly stir in cheese, remaining olive oil, and salt, to taste. Toss with hot pasta cooked until al dente.

Triple-A Pasta: Spinach Pasta with Asparagus, Artichoke, and Arugula

SERVES 4

12 ounces spinach pasta (fettuccine) or fresh
    spinach pasta, cooked until al dente
Extra-virgin olive oil, a drizzle
2 pats butter (about 1 tablespoon)
2 tablespoons extra-virgin olive oil
1 large or 2 medium shallots, finely chopped
1/2 cup white wine
1 pound thin fresh asparagus spears, washed,
    dried, and chopped (snap tough ends off,
    chop tender spears into bite-size pieces,
    cutting on an angle)
1 cup broth, chicken or vegetable
1 can (14 ounces) artichoke hearts in water,
    drained and chopped
24 leaves fresh arugula, torn or coarsely chopped
2 tablespoons lemon zest (grate the skin, not
    the white pulp of 1 large lemon)
Coarse salt and black pepper, to taste
A handful chopped fresh flat-leaf parsley,
    to garnish

Drain cooked pasta well and drizzle with a touch of oil to keep from sticking. Set aside.

Heat a large, deep skillet over medium heat. Add butter and olive oil to pan and heat until butter is melted. Add shallots and sauté, 3 minutes. Add wine and reduce liquids by half, about 2 minutes more. Add asparagus bits, cover, and cook, 3 or 4 minutes. Then uncover, adding broth and artichokes to pan. Heat artichokes through and add cooked pasta to pot. Sprinkle in arugula. Toss ingredients until arugula wilts. Season with lemon zest, salt and pepper, and parsley. Taste and adjust seasonings.

Transfer to a serving platter and serve immediately with crusty bread. Fresh sliced melon makes a simple and wonderful accompaniment before or after this meal.

Penne with Roasted Red Pepper Sauce

SERVES 4

3 roasted red peppers, homemade (see Note) or
    1 jar (14 to 16 ounces) roasted red peppers
    in water, drained
A handful fresh flat-leaf parsley
2 tablespoons extra-virgin olive oil (twice
    around the pan)
4 cloves garlic, finely chopped
Coarse salt and black pepper, to taste
1 can (28 ounces) crushed tomatoes
15 to 20 oil-cured black olives (from bulk olive
    bin of market), pitted and chopped
1 pound penne pasta, cooked until al dente
Extra-virgin olive oil, a drizzle

Place peppers and parsley in a food processor. Grind into a paste using pulse button.

Heat a deep skillet over medium heat. Add olive oil and garlic. When garlic speaks, add pepper paste; heat through and season with salt and pepper. Add tomatoes and olives. Stir until sauce bubbles. Reduce heat to low and simmer until ready to serve.

Toss hot, drained penne pasta with a drizzle olive oil and half the sauce; serve and top with additional sauce. Crusty bread and a mixed green or spinach salad complete the meal.

Note: ROASTED PEPPERS: Split red bell peppers lengthwise and seed. Place skin-side up on a cookie sheet and position under broiler on high, leaving oven door slightly ajar. Let pepper skins blacken evenly. Remove and dump peppers into a brown paper sack, close tightly, and set aside. When peppers are cool enough to handle, about 10 minutes, gently peel them.

Lentils and Pasta with Greens

SERVES 4

2/3 cup lentils, green or other variety

2 bay leaves, fresh or dried

3 tablespoons extra-virgin olive oil (3 turns around the pan, total)

1 small boiling or cooking onion, chopped

2 carrots, peeled and chopped

1/2 red bell pepper, chopped

3 cloves garlic, minced

1/2 cup red wine (a couple glugs)

2 tablespoons tomato paste

1 can (14 ounces) vegetable broth

1 pound Swiss chard, washed, dried, and chopped

1/4 teaspoon allspice (a couple pinches)

1 teaspoon ground cumin (1/3 palmful)

Coarse salt and black pepper, to taste

10 to 12 ounces pasta (bow ties or wide egg noodles), cooked until al dente

A handful chopped fresh flat-leaf parsley

Cover lentils with water and bring to a boil. Add a bay leaf and cook lentils until tender, 20 minutes. Drain and set aside.

While lentils cook, add olive oil to a hot large skillet. Add 1 bay leaf, onion, carrots, red bell pepper, and garlic. Sauté 10 minutes over medium heat. Add wine and reduce liquid for 1 minute. Stir in tomato paste and cook 1 minute more. Add vegetable broth and Swiss chard, then cover. Once greens have wilted, season with allspice, cumin, and salt and pepper, then continue cooking. Steam greens 10 minutes, until tender.

When greens are tender and no longer bitter, uncover and stir in drained pasta, lentils, and parsley. Adjust seasonings and serve.

Penne Primavera

SERVES 4

VEGETABLES:

2 cups broccoli florets, separated into bite-size pieces (ready-to-use florets are available in bulk in many produce departments)

1/2 cup shredded carrot (a couple handfuls) (pouches of shredded carrots can be found in the produce section of large markets)

1 small zucchini or yellow squash, cut into thin matchsticks

1/2 red bell pepper, seeded, and sliced into thin matchsticks

1 cup water

SAUCE:

1 tablespoon butter

1 tablespoon extra-virgin olive oil (once around the pan)

2 medium shallots, minced

2 tablespoons all-purpose flour (a palmful)

1 cup low-sodium vegetable broth (about 1/2 can)

1/2 cup half-and-half or light cream

A handful grated Parmigiano Reggiano or Romano cheese

Coarse salt and ground pepper, to taste

2 tablespoons fresh chopped thyme (a palmful)

1/2 pound penne rigate, cooked until al dente, about 8 minutes

Place vegetables in a deep skillet with 1 cup water. Bring to a simmer, cover, reduce heat to low, and steam the vegetables for 3 minutes. Drain and return to pan; cover and set aside.

In a small skillet or sauce pan melt butter into oil over medium heat. Add shallots and sauté, 2 minutes. Sprinkle with flour and cook 1 minute more. Whisk in broth and bring to a simmer to thicken. Whisk in half-and-half or light cream and bring sauce back to a bubble. Reduce heat to low and let sauce simmer uncovered, 4 or 5 minutes. Stir in cheese, salt and pepper to taste, and fresh thyme. Place vegetables back on stove top and add pasta and sauce to pan. Adjust seasonings and serve immediately.

Ratatouille Pasta

SERVES 4 TO 6

4 cloves garlic, minced

1/4 teaspoon crushed red pepper
(a couple pinches)

3 tablespoons extra-virgin olive oil (three times
around the pan)

1 small red bell pepper, seeded and chopped

1 green bell pepper or 1 cubanelle Italian
pepper, seeded and chopped

1 medium yellow-skinned onion, chopped

1 small eggplant, peeled (or skin-on, to your
taste) and diced

1 medium zucchini, coarsely diced

20 Kalamata black olives, pitted and
coarsely chopped

2 tablespoons capers (a palmful), drained

Coarse salt and black pepper, to taste

1 can (28 ounces) crushed tomatoes

A handful chopped fresh flat-leaf parsley

1/2 pound rigatoni pasta, cooked until al dente

3 ounces pine nuts (pignoli) toasted in oven
until golden (optional)

In a deep skillet or pot, working over medium heat, simmer garlic and crushed pepper in oil until the garlic speaks by sizzling in oil. Add peppers, onion, eggplant, zucchini, olives, capers, and salt and pepper. Cover pan, reduce heat to medium low, and cook the vegetables down, stirring occasionally, until eggplant begins to breakdown, about 10 to 15 minutes.

Add tomatoes and parsley and heat through. Toss with pasta and top with toasted pine nuts.

Sicilian Eggplant Marinara over Penne

SERVES 4 AS A MEAL, 8 AS A FIRST COURSE

1 medium eggplant

2 tablespoons extra-virgin olive oil (twice around the pan)

4 large cloves garlic, minced

Coarse salt and black pepper, to taste

A handful chopped fresh flat-leaf parsley

1 can (28 ounces) crushed tomatoes

20 leaves fresh basil, torn or coarsely chopped

1 pound penne rigate, cooked until al dente

Shaved or grated Parmigiano Reggiano or Asiago cheese, for topping

Preheat oven to 425 degrees F.

Cut several small slits into one side of the eggplant with the tip of a sharp knife. Place eggplant directly on oven rack in the center of the hot oven, slit-side up. Roast for 20 minutes. Remove from oven and allow to cool. Gently remove skin with a sharp knife; it should pull away easily. Using a food processor, grind the peeled eggplant into a paste and take to the stove in the processor bowl.

Heat a skillet over medium to medium-high heat. Add oil and garlic. When the garlic speaks by sizzling in oil, add eggplant paste. Season with salt and pepper to taste. Add parsley, tomatoes, and basil. Heat the sauce through and toss with cooked penne pasta. Top with grated cheese, and serve immediately.

Broccoli and Bow Ties

SERVES 4 TO 6

1 cup water

1 pound broccoli florets or broccolini florets, coarsely chopped

1/4 cup extra-virgin olive oil (4 turns around the pan)

5 cloves garlic, minced

3 pinches crushed red pepper flakes

1 pound bow-tie pasta, cooked until al dente

1/2 cup grated Parmigiano Reggiano cheese (a couple handfuls)

A handful chopped fresh flat-leaf parsley

1/4 teaspoon ground nutmeg (2 or 3 pinches)

Coarse salt and black pepper, to taste

Bring a cup of water to a boil and reduce heat to simmer. Add florets, cover pan, and steam 3 to 5 minutes, 'til tender. Drain and set aside.

Heat olive oil in a deep, nonstick skillet over medium heat. Add garlic and crushed red pepper flakes. When garlic speaks by sizzling in oil, add florets and sauté, 1 or 2 minutes. If your pan is not large enough to toss florets with pasta, transfer to a large bowl. Toss broccolini or broccoli with pasta, cheese, parsley, nutmeg, and salt and pepper. Transfer to a serving dish and serve with a green salad and crusty bread.

Northwoods Pasta

SERVES 2 TO 3

2 tablespoons extra-virgin olive oil (2 turns around the pan)

2 tablespoons butter

2 ounces fresh, mixed, wild mushrooms such as chanterelle, oyster, and shiitake (2 handfuls)

3 medium portobello mushroom caps, halved and very thinly sliced

3 cloves garlic, minced

1 cup beef broth or portobello stock (See Note)

2 sprigs rosemary, very finely chopped

2 sprigs fresh sage leaves, finely chopped or 1/2 teaspoon ground sage

1 teaspoon ground cumin (1/3 palmful)

Coarse salt and black pepper, to taste

6 ounces arugula (a bundle) washed, dried, and coarsely chopped

1/2 pound penne rigate or pennette, cooked until al dente

1/2 cup grated pepato, Romano, or Asiago cheese

Heat olive oil and butter over medium heat in a large skillet. Add mushrooms and garlic, sauté 2 minutes, then cover pan. Cook 10 to 15 minutes, stirring occasionally, until the mushrooms are tender and dark; juices that look like beef gravy will gather in the pan. Remove cover and add broth. Bring broth to a boil, add rosemary, sage, cumin, and salt and pepper and reduce, 5 minutes. Remove from heat, add arugula, pasta, and cheese. Toss until combined and serve immediately.

Note: See recipe for Portobello stock, page 60.

Green Gnocchi

SERVES 4

2 tablespoons extra-virgin olive oil (2 turns around the pan)

1 medium onion, finely chopped

3 cloves garlic, finely chopped

1 cup vegetable broth

1 package (10 ounces) frozen chopped spinach, defrosted, drained and squeezed dry

1 cup basil leaves, loosely packed (about 20 leaves)

1/2 cup fresh flat-leaf parsley (a couple handfuls)

1 pound potato gnocchi, cooked to directions on package

1/2 cup grated Romano cheese

Coarse salt and black pepper, to taste

2 ounces pine nuts (a handful), lightly toasted, to garnish

Heat a deep skillet over medium meat. Add olive oil, onion, and garlic and sauté, 3 minutes. Add broth and reduce heat to low.

Grind spinach in a food processor. Remove and set aside. Add basil and parsley to processor and pulse-grind until very finely chopped.

Toss hot, cooked gnocchi with broth and onions. Add spinach and heat through. Remove pan from heat and stir in basil, parsley, and Romano cheese. Season with salt and pepper, to taste. Garnish with toasted pine nuts and serve.

Eggplant Parmigiano

SERVES 2

1 small, firm eggplant or 3 baby eggplants
(see Note)

1/2 cup all-purpose flour

3 large eggs or 1 cup pasteurized egg substitute

1 1/2 cups bread crumbs, plain

2 to 3 sprigs fresh rosemary, very finely chopped
(about 2 tablespoons)

3 to 4 sprigs fresh thyme leaves, finely chopped

A handful fresh flat-leaf parsley, finely chopped

1/2 to 2/3 cup grated Parmigiano Reggiano
cheese (a couple handfuls)

2 pinches coarse salt

Freshly ground black pepper, to taste

4 to 6 tablespoons extra-virgin olive oil (4 turns
around the pan), total

4 pats butter (about 1/2 tablespoon each),
2 tablespoons total

1 recipe 15-Minute Marinara (recipe follows) or
1 quart jarred sauce

Serving suggestions:

1/2 pound fresh pasta cooked until al dente and
tossed with a drizzle of olive oil or crusty
semolina bread

For eggplant capped with melted cheese:

1/2 pound fresh or smoked mozzarella, thinly
sliced or shaved Asiago or sliced provolone
cheese

Preheat oven to 300 degrees F and place a cookie sheet on the center rack.

Slice eggplants lengthwise 1/4-inch thick. Place flour in a shallow dish. Beat eggs or egg substitute with a splash of water and pour into a shallow bowl. Set bowl next to flour dish. In a third shallow bowl or platter, combine bread crumbs, herbs, cheese, and salt and pepper.

Heat a large skillet over medium heat. Add 2 tablespoons olive oil (twice around the pan) and 1 pat of butter. When butter has melted into the oil, begin coating eggplant in flour, then egg, and then bread crumbs, adding coated slices to pan. Cook in batches in single layers, adding a little more oil and another pat of butter to pan with each batch. Brown eggplant slices about 2 minutes on each side 'til golden, then transfer to oven to finish cooking, about 5 to 10 minutes. Top with a little Marinara Sauce and serve with crusty bread and a green salad.

Note: Baby eggplants, marked Sicilian and Japanese, are not as bitter or as porous as their bigger relatives. They need not be salted and pressed before cooking, a time-saving advantage if you crave eggplant parmigiano and don't have a lot of time to make it.

Variation

For a quick casserole, layer sauce and eggplant in a shallow dish and melt fresh or smoked mozzarella, Asiago or provolone cheese under the broiler on high until cheese begins to brown at the edges.

15-Minute Marinara Sauce

2 to 3 tablespoons extra-virgin olive oil (2 or 3 turns around the pan)
4 large cloves garlic, finely chopped
2 or 3 pinches crushed red pepper flakes
1 can (28 ounces) whole tomatoes, seeded and coarsely chopped
1 can (28 ounces) crushed tomatoes
2 sprigs fresh oregano, finely chopped (about 1 tablespoon)
A handful fresh flat-leaf parsley, finely chopped
12 to 15 leaves fresh basil, stacked, rolled into logs, and thinly sliced
Coarse salt and black pepper, to taste

Heat a deep skillet over medium to medium-low heat. Add oil and garlic and crushed pepper flakes. Let garlic begin to speak (sizzle in oil), stirring frequently to keep garlic from browning and turning bitter. Add whole and crushed tomatoes. Stir in herbs and spices and let sauce come to a boil. Reduce heat to low and simmer 10 minutes or until ready to serve.

Elsa's Eggplant Roll-ups

SERVES 4

Vegetable or olive oil, for frying

2 medium eggplants (Sicilian variety, smaller
    than regular, bigger than Japanese)

3/4 cup flour (a couple handfuls)

Coarse salt and black pepper, to taste

3 eggs beaten, or 3/4 cup pasteurized egg
    substitute

FILLING:

1 pound fresh mozzarella, or fresh smoked
    mozzarella, diced

20 leaves fresh basil

2 cups marinara sauce, homemade or jarred

Chopped fresh parsley, for garnish

Heat 1/2 inch of oil in a large skillet over medium-high heat.

Thinly slice eggplants lengthwise. Place flour in a shallow dish and season with salt and pepper. Dredge slices lightly in flour, then coat in egg and place in heated pan. Fry 2 minutes on each side until golden, then transfer to paper towel-lined plate to drain.

Drain excess oil from pan, wipe, and return to heat.

Top each eggplant slice with a leaf of fresh basil and diced cheese and roll-up slice. Place bundles back in pan. Top with marinara sauce. Reduce heat to low. Cover and cook 8 minutes. Top with parsley and serve.

Vegetable Barley

SERVES 3

This dish is so warm and hearty that you will need a place to curl up and nap after eating it.

4 cups chicken or vegetable broth
1 tablespoon extra-virgin olive oil (2 turns
    around the pan)
1 tablespoon butter
1/2 cup barley
1 small carrot, peeled and finely diced
1 small rib of celery from the heart of the stalk,
    finely diced
1 small onion, finely diced
1 bay leaf, fresh or dried
Coarse salt, to taste
1/4 teaspoon allspice (a few pinches)
10 ounces fresh spinach, trimmed and steamed

Pour broth into a small pot and place over low heat to warm.

Melt olive oil and butter in a medium pot over medium heat. Add barley and cook 3 minutes, stirring frequently. Add veggies and bay leaf and season with salt and allspice. Sauté mixture, 3 minutes longer. Add warm broth and bring to a boil. Reduce heat to simmer, cover, and cook until barley is tender, about 12 minutes.

To serve, pile mounds of vegetable barley on beds of steamed spinach.

Cauliflower Au Gratin

SERVES 4

1 large head cauliflower
3 tablespoons butter
3 tablespoons flour
1 cup reduced-fat milk or vegetable broth
$1/4$ teaspoon ground or freshly grated nutmeg
    (a few pinches)
Coarse salt and black pepper, to taste
1 $1/2$ cups shredded Gruyère cheese (8 ounces)

Remove leaves from stem of cauliflower and wash. Cut around core of cauliflower with a paring knife and remove it, leaving head whole. Place 3 to 4 cups water in a large deep pot and set the cauliflower into the pot. Cover, and bring to a boil over medium-high heat. Reduce heat to medium low and steam, 10 minutes.

Place rack in center of broiler oven and preheat to high.

Heat a small sauce pan over medium heat. Melt butter and whisk in flour. Whisk for 3 minutes to form a roux. Add milk or broth in a slow stream to combine with roux. Reduce heat to low.

Transfer steamed cauliflower to a large casserole dish. Using a paring knife, separate florets and turn right-side up. Sprinkle with half of the grated Gruyère.

Remove $1/2$ cup of the cooking water used to steam cauliflower and whisk into sauce. Season with nutmeg, salt, and pepper to taste. Pour sauce over florets and top with remaining cheese. Place casserole under broiler and cook until cheese is brown and bubbly, about 3 to 5 minutes.

Polenta with Sun-Dried Tomato Sauce

SERVES 2

2 ounces sun-dried tomatoes (about 3/4 cup)

1 roll (16 ounces) prepared polenta, available in produce or dairy aisles of market

2 tablespoons extra-virgin olive oil (2 turns around the pan)

2 or 3 sprigs fresh thyme, finely chopped, or a few pinches dried thyme

Coarse salt and black pepper, to taste

1 small onion, finely chopped

3 cloves garlic, crushed and minced

1 can (14 ounces) crushed tomatoes or chunky-style crushed tomatoes

1 1/2 cups shredded fontina cheese

Bring a small pot half-full with water to a boil. Add sun-dried tomatoes, simmer, 10 minutes, and set aside.

Slice polenta into 1/2-inch thick discs.

Heat 1 tablespoon olive oil in a large nonstick skillet over medium-high heat. Arrange polenta in a single layer in the pan and season with thyme, salt, and pepper. Pan fry, 3 minutes on each side. Remove and arrange in a serving dish. Reduce heat to medium low and return pan to heat. Add 1 tablespoon olive oil, onion, and garlic. Sauté 3 minutes, stirring occasionally.

Preheat broiler to high and place rack in center of oven.

Remove sun-dried tomatoes from water, coarsely chop, and place in a small bowl. Add onion and garlic, and stir in crushed tomatoes.

Spoon sauce over polenta and cover with a layer of shredded cheese. Place serving dish in oven 'til cheese bubbles and begins to brown.

Polenta with Roasted Vegetable Sauce

SERVES 3

1 small zucchini, trimmed and diced

1 medium onion, peeled and diced

1 baby eggplant, trimmed and diced

4 cloves garlic, crushed

Extra-virgin olive oil, for drizzling (about 2 tablespoons)

2 or 3 sprigs fresh rosemary, leaves stripped from stems and finely chopped

Coarse salt and black pepper, to taste

1 roll (16 ounces) prepared polenta or flavored polenta

Cooking spray or extra-virgin olive oil, to coat polenta

1 can (14 ounces) crushed tomatoes

Asiago, pepato or crushed red pepper grating cheese, for garnish

Preheat oven to 500 degrees F.

Combine diced zucchini, onion, eggplant, and crushed garlic in a bowl. Drizzle with olive oil to lightly coat vegetables. Season with rosemary, salt and pepper, and gently toss to combine. Spread as an even layer on a nonstick cookie sheet and roast, 10 to 12 minutes or until tender.

Slice polenta into 1/2-inch thick discs. Spray a separate baking sheet with cooking spray or brush discs with a little olive oil. Arrange on baking sheet in a single layer, sprinkle with a little coarse salt, and roast, along with veggies.

Warm crushed tomatoes in a medium pan over medium heat. Add roasted vegetables and toss to coat evenly. On a serving dish, layer polenta slices with ladles of roasted vegetables and garnish with shaved Asiago, pepato or crushed red pepper cheese.

Garden Pasta

SERVES 4 TO 6

Leftovers only get better.

2 tablespoons extra-virgin olive oil (twice around the pan)

4 cloves garlic, minced

1 medium zucchini, finely diced

1 small yellow-skinned onion, finely chopped

1 small carrot, finely chopped

2 bay leaves, fresh or dried

1/2 cup vegetable or chicken broth (a couple of splashes)

1 can (28 ounces) crushed tomatoes

Coarse salt and black pepper, to taste

A handful chopped fresh flat-leaf parsley (2 or 3 tablespoons)

1 pound penne rigate, cooked until al dente

4 scallions, thinly sliced, for garnish (optional)

Heat a deep skillet or pot over medium heat. Add oil and garlic and sauté, until the garlic sizzles. Add zucchini, onion, carrot, and bay leaves. Cover and cook, 5 minutes, stirring occasionally, or until zucchini is tender and onions are translucent. Remove cover and add broth. Stir up any good gunk from the bottom of the pot. Add tomatoes, salt and pepper, parsley, and bring to a bubble. Reduce heat to low and simmer until ready to serve. Combine sauce with pasta and garnish with chopped scallions.

Herb Fettuccini

SERVES 4

1/2 cup extra-virgin olive oil (5 turns around
   the pan)

1 pound fresh fettuccini or egg fettuccini,
   cooked until al dente

1/4 cup chopped fresh flat-leaf parsley
   (2 handfuls)

20 leaves fresh basil, stacked, rolled into logs,
   and thinly sliced

6 sprigs fresh tarragon, leaves stripped from
   stems and chopped

4 to 6 sprigs fresh mint, leaves chopped

2 or 3 sprigs fresh marjoram, chopped or a
   few pinches dried

6 sprigs fresh thyme, leaves stripped from
   stems and chopped

4 sprigs fresh sage, leaves chopped (about
   2 tablespoons)

2 sprigs fresh rosemary, leaves stripped and
   finely chopped

2 fresh, firm vine-ripe tomatoes, seeded
   and diced

Coarse salt and black pepper, to taste

1/2 cup grated Parmigiano Reggiano or Romano
   cheese (a couple handfuls)

Warm olive oil. Toss drained, hot pasta with warm oil, herbs, tomatoes, salt and pepper, and cheese. Serve with salad and crusty bread. Yum.

Make Your Own Asian Take-Out

Chinese and Thai-Style Vegetable Dinners

Though take-out Asian foods are full of colorful veggies, they may also contain large amounts of fat, salt, and MSG.

I love take-out anything, but when I make my own, I control the fat and salt content. By crafting a more healthful lo mein that's heavy on the veggies and easy on the noodles, I feel better about eating my fill.

Remember, too, that these are 30-minute meals (beats a delivery), and I call for ingredients found in most supermarkets, and use them economically in more than one recipe. Wok on!

Garlic Ginger Vegetable Stir-Fry

SERVES 2

1 cup white rice, prepared to directions
    on package

1 tablespoon vegetable or wok oil (1 turn around
    the pan)
2 teaspoons dark sesame oil (a couple drizzles)
1/2 head small Nappa cabbage, shredded
1/4 pound snow peas (a couple handfuls),
    trimmed and cut in half on an angle
1 red bell pepper, seeded, quartered lengthwise
    and sliced into thin strips across
5 scallions, thinly sliced on an angle
2 cups bean sprouts, washed and drained
3 cloves garlic, finely chopped
2 inches fresh gingerroot, finely chopped
    or grated
1/4 cup dark soy sauce (Tamari)
1 tablespoon Chinese 5-spice powder
Juice of 1 large navel orange
3 ounces apricot preserves (about 3 rounded
    tablespoons)
Coarse salt, to taste

Prepare rice, and start to cook.

Heat a large nonstick skillet over high heat. Add vegetable or wok oil and sesame oil to hot pan. Add vegetables and stir-fry, 2 or 3 minutes. Add garlic and ginger and stir-fry, 2 minutes more. Add soy sauce, 3 turns around the pan in a slow stream. Sprinkle with Chinese 5-spice powder. Juice orange over pan, then add preserves. Remove pan from heat and toss until vegetables are evenly coated and preserves dissolved. Season with a few pinches of salt, to taste, and serve over white rice.

Cashew Vegetables
SERVES 2 TO 3

1 cup white or jasmine rice, cooked to directions
    on package

1 pound broccoli tops, separated into
    small florets
1 tablespoon wok or vegetable oil
1 medium onion, thinly sliced
4 ounces snow peas (a couple handfuls),
    trimmed of tips
1 small red bell pepper, seeded and thinly sliced
1 can (14 ounces) baby corn, drained
2 to 3 ounces (2 rounded tablespoons) hoisin
    sauce (found on Asian foods aisle)
4 ounces duck sauce (4 rounded tablespoons)
4 ounces unsalted cashews (a couple handfuls
    from the bulk bins)
Coarse salt, to taste
Crushed red pepper flakes (optional)

Prepare rice and start to cook.

Bring a small pot of water to a boil. Add broccoli and cook, 2 to 3 minutes. Drain well.

Heat a deep nonstick skillet or wok-shaped pan over high heat. To the hot pan, add oil and onions. Cook 1 or 2 minutes, then add broccoli, snow peas, bell pepper, and baby corn. Stir-fry veggies, 3 or 4 minutes. Add hoisin and duck sauces and toss until veggies are evenly coated. Remove from heat and toss with cashews. Season with salt and a little crushed red pepper flakes, if you like it spicy. Serve over hot cooked rice.

Thai Spicy Eggplant with Sweet Basil
SERVES 2 TO 3

1 cup jasmine rice, cooked to directions on
the package

2 tablespoons wok, peanut or vegetable oil
(2 turns around the pan)
1/2 to 1 teaspoon crushed red pepper flakes,
depending on how hot you like it
3 baby eggplant, cubed into bite-size chunks
1 medium onion, diced
1 medium red bell pepper, seeded and diced
4 cloves garlic, finely chopped
2 tablespoons fish sauce or white vinegar
(2 splashes)
3 tablespoons dark soy sauce, Tamari (3 turns
around the pan)
2 tablespoons dark brown sugar (a palmful)
20 leaves fresh basil, shredded or torn

Prepare rice, and start to cook.

Heat a deep skillet or wok-shaped pan over
high heat. Add oil, crushed pepper flakes, and
let sizzle, 10 to 15 seconds. Add eggplant and
stir-fry, 2 to 3 minutes. Add onion, bell pepper,
and garlic, and stir-fry another 3 minutes. Add
fish sauce and soy. Then sprinkle with sugar
and toss, 1 or 2 minutes longer. Remove pan
from heat, add basil leaves, and toss to combine
with eggplant. Serve over hot cooked rice.

Sesame Green Beans

SERVES 2 AS AN ENTRÉE, 4 AS A SIDE DISH

1 cup Jasmine or white rice, cooked to directions
    on package

1 pound fresh green beans, washed and trimmed
1 1/2 to 2 tablespoons dark sesame oil (2 turns
    around the pan)
Juice of 1 orange
2 tablespoons toasted sesame seeds (a palmful)
Coarse salt, to taste
Soy sauce, for the table

Prepare rice, and start to cook.

Bring an inch of water in a skillet to a simmer. Add green beans, cover, and steam, 3 minutes. Run under cold water and drain well.

Heat a skillet or wok-shaped pan over high heat. Add oil, then beans, and stir-fry, 2 minutes. Squeeze the orange juice evenly over the beans, sprinkle with sesame seeds, and season with salt, to taste. Serve with Jasmine or white rice and soy sauce, for drizzling.

Spicy Green Beans

SERVES 2 AS AN ENTRÉE, 4 AS A SIDE DISH

1 cup white or Jasmine rice, cooked to directions
on package

1 pound fresh green beans, washed and trimmed

1 1/2 to 2 tablespoons dark sesame oil (2 turns
around the pan)

1/2 small onion, thinly sliced

1 small red bell pepper, sliced into thin strips

3 cloves garlic, minced

1/4 to 1/2 teaspoon crushed red pepper flakes
(medium to hot)

1 inch fresh gingerroot, grated or minced

Juice of 1 orange

3 ounces (2 rounded tablespoons) hoisin sauce
(found in Asian foods aisle)

2 ounces slivered almonds, lightly toasted,
for garnish

Prepare rice.

Steam green beans in simmering water, 3 minutes, covered. Rinse in cool water, then drain very well.

Place a large skillet over high heat. Add oil, then onion and bell pepper, and stir-fry, 1 or 2 minutes. Add garlic, crushed pepper, ginger, and beans, and stir-fry, 1 minute more. Squeeze orange juice over the pan, add hoisin sauce, and toss to coat evenly with sauce. Serve with toasted almonds and Jasmine or white rice.

Curried Eggplant and Jasmine Rice

SERVES 3 TO 4

1 1/2 cups Jasmine rice, cooked to directions
   on package

2 tablespoons extra-virgin olive oil
1 medium eggplant or 3 baby eggplant, cubed
1 large yellow-skinned onion, chopped
1 small red bell pepper, seeded and diced
4 cloves garlic, minced
1 can (14 ounces) diced tomatoes, drained
1/4 cup (a couple heaping tablespoons)
   mango chutney
A palmful curry powder (about 2 tablespoons)
   or 1 rounded tablespoon curry paste
Coarse salt, to taste
1 cup vegetable broth
A palmful fresh cilantro leaves, finely
   chopped (optional)

Suggested garnishes:
Toasted slivered almonds
Thinly sliced scallions

Prepare rice, and start to cook.

Heat a deep skillet over medium to medium-high heat. When the pan is hot, add olive oil, eggplant, onion, and bell pepper. Cook for 6 to 8 minutes, covered, stirring occasionally. Uncover and add garlic; cook 1 minute more. Add tomatoes, chutney, curry powder, a couple pinches salt, and broth. Stir to combine completely, and let simmer, another 5 minutes. Remove from heat and add cilantro. Pour over rice and garnish with toasted almonds and scallions.

Veggie Lo Mein

SERVES 4

2 tablespoons vegetable or wok oil (twice
   around the pan)
2 cups (4 handfuls) fresh snow peas
1 small red bell pepper, seeded and cut into thin
   matchsticks
4 scallions, thinly sliced on an angle
1 cup (a couple handfuls) fresh bean
   sprouts (optional)
1 inch peeled gingerroot, grated or minced
3 or 4 cloves garlic, minced
$1/2$ to $3/4$ pound thin spaghetti, cooked until
   al dente and drained
$1/2$ cup aged Tamari soy sauce
2 tablespoons toasted sesame oil (several shakes)
Coarse salt, to taste

Heat a wok-shaped skillet or large, nonstick skillet over high heat. When pan is hot, add oil—it will smoke a bit—then, immediately add vegetables and stir-fry, 2 or 3 minutes. Add ginger and garlic, continue stir-frying 1 minute longer, then add pasta and combine with vegetables until evenly distributed. Add Tamari sauce (remove shaker top, and go 4 turns around the pan in a slow stream) and toss, until evenly coated. Transfer to a platter, drizzle with sesame oil, adding salt, to taste, and serve.

Snack Suppers

Stuffed Potatoes, Sandwiches, Dips, and Spreads

My idea of a perfect day-off begins with a heavy rain or snowfall; I'm trapped, and can't possibly run those errands or make that meeting 50 miles away.

What do I do? I bundle up in layers of my favorite tees and flannels, whip up a tray of snacks, and nestle in to watch video after video, with my trusty dog, Boo, warming my feet and eating my leftovers.

When the next storm hits or when you crave a simple supper, make yourself a veggie snack. Spinach calzone, pita-pizza or stuffed potato anyone?

Potato Toppers

EACH OF THE FOLLOWING RECIPES WILL TOP 4 LARGE BAKED POTATOES.

To quick-bake potatoes, preheat oven to 450 degrees F.

To prepare potatoes, pierce in several spots with the tines of a fork. Rub skins with a touch of vegetable or extra-virgin olive oil, and microwave on high for 8 minutes, turning once. Wrap potatoes in foil, place on center rack of preheated oven, and roast, 20 minutes. Split and top with fixings of choice.

Broccoli Cheese Stuffed Potatoes
SERVES 4

4 large Russet or Idaho potatoes, baked

1 pound fresh broccoli florets or chopped broccolini (looks like a bundle of florets with thin stems)

1/3 cup water

1 tablespoon vegetable or canola oil (once around the pan)

1 pat butter (about 2 teaspoons)

1 large shallot, finely chopped

A handful flour (about 2 tablespoons)

1 cup vegetable or fat-free chicken broth

10 to 12 ounces shredded herb, dill, or onion cheddar (such as Cabot brand, about 2 1/2 cups)

Coarse salt and black pepper, to taste

12 blades fresh chives, chopped, for garnish

Steam broccoli in 1/3 cup water in a covered pot for 5 minutes. Remove from heat, drain, and let stand.

Heat vegetable oil in a small sauce pan over medium heat. Add butter and melt into oil. Add shallot and sauté, 3 minutes. Sprinkle with flour and cook, 1 minute more. Whisk in broth and stir constantly, until broth begins to thicken. Add cheese, continuing to whisk until a smooth sauce forms.

Return broccoli to pan and cover with sauce. Season with salt and pepper, to taste.

Top baked potatoes with broccoli and cheese sauce, and garnish with chopped chives.

Tomato, Eggplant, and Red Onion-Topped Potatoes
SERVES 4

4 large Russet or Idaho potatoes, baked

2 tablespoons extra-virgin olive oil (twice around the pan)
1 small red onion, chopped
A splash red wine vinegar (a few shakes)
1 baby eggplant, diced
2 vine-ripe tomatoes, seeded and diced
1/2 teaspoon ground cumin (a few healthy pinches)
1 teaspoon sugar
Coarse salt and black pepper, to taste
16 leaves fresh basil, shredded

Heat a medium nonstick skillet over medium heat. Add olive oil, then red onion, and sauté, 3 minutes. Add vinegar and deglaze pan. Add eggplant, cover, and reduce heat to medium low. Cook 6 to 8 minutes, stirring occasionally, 'til tender. Remove cover, add tomatoes, and toss with eggplant to combine. Season with cumin, sugar, and salt and pepper. Adjust seasonings. Top baked potatoes with tomato-eggplant sauce and garnish with lots of shredded basil.

3-Mushroom and Fontina-Stuffed Potatoes
SERVES 4

4 large Russet or Idaho potatoes, baked

1/2 ounce dried porcini mushrooms

1 cup water

2 tablespoons extra-virgin olive oil (twice around the pan)

1 large shallot, finely chopped

2 medium portobello mushroom caps, halved and thinly sliced

8 fresh Shiitake mushrooms, thinly sliced

Coarse salt and black pepper, to taste

10 ounces fontina cheese, shredded (about 2¹/₂ cups)

4 sprigs fresh thyme, stripped of leaves and chopped (about 1 tablespoon)

12 blades fresh chives, chopped or 2 scallions, thinly sliced, to garnish

Place porcini mushrooms in 1 cup water in a small saucepan and bring to a boil. Reduce heat to low and let simmer, about 10 minutes or until tender.

Add olive oil to a medium nonstick skillet over medium heat. Add shallots and sauté, 2 minutes. Add sliced portobellos. Cover and cook, 6 or 7 minutes, until mushrooms are dark and tender.

Remove porcini mushrooms from their liquid and slice.

Add porcinis to the portobello mushrooms. Slice fresh shiitakes and add to pan. Toss and continue cooking, 2 or 3 minutes more. Season with salt and pepper, to taste.

Pile mushrooms on split baked potatoes. Top with shredded fontina cheese and chopped thyme. Brown under broiler until bubbly and golden. Garnish with fresh chives or scallions.

Chilied Veggies-Topped Potatoes
SERVES 4

4 large Idaho potatoes, baked

1 tablespoon vegetable or corn oil (once around
the pan)
1 green bell pepper, seeded and diced
1 medium sweet onion, diced
2 cloves garlic, peeled and minced
1 jalapeño pepper, seeded and finely chopped
1 can (14 ounces) diced tomatoes
 Half a palmful cilantro, chopped (about 1
tablespoon)
1 teaspoon dark chili powder ($^1/_3$ palmful)
1 teaspoon ground cumin ($^1/_3$ palmful)
Coarse salt, to taste
A few drops cayenne pepper sauce (such as
Tabasco or Red Hot brands)
8 ounces shredded Monterey Jack or Pepper
Jack cheese (optional)
2 scallions, thinly sliced, for garnish

Heat a nonstick skillet over medium-high heat. Add oil, bell pepper, and onion. Sauté, stirring frequently, 3 to 5 minutes, until veggies start to brown at the edges. Add garlic and jalapeño, and cook 1 minute more. Add tomatoes and cilantro, then season with chili powder, cumin, salt, and pepper sauce. Reduce heat and simmer a few minutes more to combine flavors.

Remove from heat and top split, baked potatoes with the veggies. Sprinkle cheese, if you like, and brown under hot broiler until bubbly. Garnish with sliced scallions.

Broccoli Rabe Melts

MAKES 2 GRINDERS

1 to 1 1/2 pounds broccoli rabe (1 large bunch)

2 tablespoons extra-virgin olive oil (twice around the pan)

2 cloves garlic, popped from skin and finely chopped

A few pinches crushed red pepper flakes (about 1/4 teaspoon)

Coarse salt, to taste

1 loaf garlic bread, homemade or store-bought

8 ounces smoked mozzarella or provolone cheese, thinly sliced

Heat a medium pot with 2 or 3 quarts water to boiling. Chop broccoli rabe tops into 1-inch pieces, discarding stems, and any discolored leaves. Place tops into water and boil, 5 minutes. Drain well.

Heat a nonstick skillet over medium heat. Add olive oil, garlic, and crushed pepper flakes. When garlic speaks by sizzling in oil, add broccoli rabe and sauté, 2 or 3 minutes. Remove from heat and season with a little salt, to taste.

Lightly brown garlic bread under broiler on a cookie sheet. Pile greens across one-half of the entire loaf. Top with cheese and place under broiler to melt cheese. Remove and replace the top half. Cut the entire loaf into 2 big wedges.

Enjoy with a tomato and onion salad and a good bottle of Italian wine. Life does not get much better than this.

Eggplant and Mozzarella Melts

MAKES 4 MELTS

1 whole bulb of garlic cloves
8 slices eggplant (1/2-inch thick)
Olive-oil cooking spray
Coarse salt and black pepper, to taste
8 slices crusty, firm semolina bread (1/2-inch thick)
4 ounces sliced fresh mozzarella or fresh
    smoked mozzarella cheese (4, 1/4-inch
    thick slices)
4 thick slices large vine-ripe tomato
20 leaves fresh basil
1 ounce mixed baby greens
A drizzle extra-virgin olive oil (1 tablespoon)
A sprinkle balsamic vinegar (1 1/2 teaspoons)

Prepare outdoor grill on medium heat or preheat a grill pan or large nonstick skillet over medium to medium-high heat.

Cut the bulb of garlic at the base, exposing the ends of each clove. Spray generously with cooking spray and wrap tightly in foil, making a pouch. Place garlic on grill to roast 20 minutes, turning packet occasionally. For indoor preparation, place pouch in a small skillet with a tight lid and pan-roast, covered, 15 minutes, turning once. Let garlic cool, 3 minutes and squeeze cloves out of their skins. Mash into a paste.

Spray both sides of eggplant slices with cooking oil and season with a little salt and pepper. Lightly spray grill or pan with oil and grill eggplant, 8 minutes, turning occasionally.

Spray bread lightly on each side and grill alongside eggplant for the last 2 to 3 minutes, toasting until golden on each side with indirect heat. For indoor preparation, broil bread a minute on each side in oven or toaster oven, until golden and crisp.

When eggplant is tender, place a slice of cheese on each of 4 slices of eggplant and top with remaining eggplant. When cheese begins to melt, remove from grill and top each stack with a slice of tomato.

Toss basil and baby greens with a little oil and vinegar, salt and pepper.

To assemble sandwiches, spread garlic paste across semolina toast slice, top with greens, eggplant, mozzarella, and tomato and another slice of toast.

Open-Faced Eggplant and Tomato Melt
MAKES 2 MELTS

1 1/2 ounces pine nuts (a handful)

3 tablespoons extra-virgin olive oil (3 turns around the pan)

1 small eggplant or 2 baby eggplants, peeled and diced

Coarse salt and black pepper, to taste

1/2 teaspoon ground cumin (a few good pinches)

1 vine-ripened tomato, seeded and diced

6 ounces ricotta salata cheese, crumbled

10 leaves fresh basil

1/2 loaf crusty baguette, split lengthwise

Heat a medium nonstick skillet over medium heat. Add pine nuts and lightly toast, stirring or shaking pan frequently. Remove nuts and set aside to cool. Return pan to heat.

Add olive oil to the hot pan. Add eggplant and cover. Cook 6 minutes, until tender, stirring occasionally. Remove cover and season with salt, pepper, and cumin.

Combine diced tomato and crumbled ricotta salata. Pile leaves of basil one atop another, then roll lengthwise into a log. Thinly slice the log, creating a basil confetti.

To assemble, place 2 halves of baguette on a cookie sheet. Pile bread with eggplant and top with cheese and tomato. Place cookie sheet under hot broiler until edges of cheese and bread begin to brown and cheese starts to melt. Remove and top with lots of basil confetti and toasted pine nuts. Ohhh-yeah!

Portobello Pizza Burgers

SERVES 4

4 medium portobello mushroom caps (about
the size of a burger)

3 tablespoons extra-virgin olive oil (a couple glugs)

1 1/2 tablespoons balsamic vinegar or white
balsamic vinegar (a couple splashes)

2 sprigs fresh oregano, chopped (3 pinches dried)

A couple shakes crushed red pepper flakes

Montreal Steak Seasoning, by McCormick or
coarse salt, pepper, and a pinch garlic powder

4 ounces pizza sauce

4 ounces sliced smoked fresh mozzarella or
sliced sharp provolone cheese

4 crusty round rolls, split

Wash and dry portobello caps.

Combine olive oil, vinegar, oregano, and crushed red pepper flakes in a large, plastic food storage bag. Add mushrooms, seal bag and coat caps with a good shake of the bag.

Heat a grill pan or outdoor grill to medium-high heat. Cook mushroom caps, 6 minutes on each side, starting top-side-up and flipping to cap-side down.

Heat pizza sauce in a small pan over low heat or on top of outdoor grill.

Drain off excess juices that accumulate in the caps.

Top each cap with sauce and cheese. Close grill or place aluminum foil tent over pan to melt cheese. Place portobello pizzas on a crusty roll and enjoy with a spinach salad and specialty potato or root vegetable chips.

Portobello Parmigiano Sandwiches with Roasted Pepper Salsa

SERVES 4

These are good, real good.

1/2 cup Italian bread crumbs

1/2 cup wheat germ

1/2 cup grated Parmigiano Reggiano or
      Parmesan cheese

2 sprigs each, fresh rosemary and thyme, finely
      chopped or a few pinches each, dried
      rosemary and thyme leaves, crumbled

Black pepper, to taste

2 eggs, beaten or 1/2 cup egg substitute

A splash skim milk or water

4 medium portobello mushroom caps, cleaned
      and dried

Olive oil cooking spray

4 whole grain rolls, split

4 slices fresh or smoked mozzarella

TOPPING:

4 ounces jarred roasted red peppers, drained

4 ounces pizza sauce

FIXINGS:

Red onion, (thinly sliced), tomato, and baby
      spinach greens

Combine bread crumbs, wheat germ, cheese, herbs, and pepper in a large food storage bag.

Beat eggs with a splash of water or milk.

Coat mushrooms in egg. Shake off excess and drop mushrooms, 1 at a time, into bag and shake to coat. Repeat for all 4 caps. Spray caps on both sides with cooking spray.

Heat a large nonstick skillet to medium-high heat or preheat a cookie sheet placed on the middle rack of a 400 degree F oven. In a skillet, place coated mushrooms stem side down and dry roast caps 6 minutes on each side, placing a loose foil tent over pan. If caps brown too quickly, reduce heat a little. Cook until tender and golden, 12 to 15 minutes. In oven, roast stem side down, 15 to 18 minutes. In either method, melt cheese over the tops in the last minute.

Combine peppers and pizza sauce in food processor and pulse grind until a smooth paste forms.

Pile portobellos on buns and top with spread, tomato, onion, and spinach. Serve with chips or oven fries.

Portobello Burgers
with Roasted Pepper Spread

MAKES 4 "BURGERS"

4 medium portobello mushroom caps

MARINADE:

3 splashes balsamic vinegar (2 to 3 tablespoons)

3 tablespoons extra-virgin olive oil

4 or 5 dashes Worcestershire sauce

2 sprigs fresh rosemary, leaves stripped from
    stem and minced

Montreal Steak Seasoning by McCormick or
    coarse salt and black pepper, to taste

4 slices provolone cheese or 6 ounces fresh
    smoked mozzarella, thinly sliced

ROASTED PEPPER SPREAD:

1 jar (14 ounces) roasted red pepper, drained, or
    3 homemade roasted peppers

1 clove garlic, cracked from skin

A drizzle extra-virgin olive oil

A handful fresh flat-leaf parsley

A pinch coarse salt and black pepper, to taste

4 pieces Romaine lettuce or arugula

4 thin slices red onion (optional)

4 crusty hard rolls (Kaiser or Italian club rolls,
    sesame-seeded or plain), split and toasted

Yukon Gold or other premium chips, for
    garnish (optional)

SUGGESTED SIDE DISH:
Tomatoes, cucumbers, and onions, chunked and
dressed with oil and vinegar

Quickly rinse and pat dry caps, set aside.
Combine marinade, except Montreal Seasoning,
in a large plastic food storage bag. Add mushroom caps, seal, and shake to evenly coat.

Heat a nonstick griddle or skillet over medium-high heat. Add portobellos and cook, 3 to 5
minutes on each side, turning once; caps should
be tender and dark. Place a slice of cheese on
each cap and remove from heat.

Combine ingredients for the roasted red pepper
spread in a food processor and pulse until a
paste is formed.

Toast rolls lightly under broiler or in toaster
oven. Spread generously with roasted pepper.
Pile "burgers" in this order: bottom of roll, portobello with cheese, Romaine or arugula leaves,
red onion slice, and roll top. Garnish with
fancy chips, like Yukon Gold onion and garlic
chips by Terra brand, or, with a nice chunked
vegetable salad.

Spinach Calzones

MAKES 4 CALZONES

2 cups part-skim low-moisture ricotta cheese

$1/2$ teaspoon ground nutmeg (a few pinches) or freshly grated

Coarse salt and black pepper, to taste

A handful grated Parmigiano Reggiano cheese (about 3 tablespoons)

1 package (10 ounces) frozen chopped spinach, defrosted and squeezed dry

1 jar (7 ounces) roasted red peppers, drained and chopped

2 cloves garlic, finely chopped

Cooking spray

1 can (10 ounces) refrigerated pizza crust, available on dairy aisle

1 cup shredded part-skim mozzarella cheese (5 ounces)

2 cups marinara sauce, homemade or jarred

Preheat oven to 425 degrees F.

Season ricotta with nutmeg, salt, and pepper. In a medium bowl, combine ricotta, Parmigiano, spinach, roasted peppers, and garlic.

Spray cookie sheet with cooking spray. Roll dough out and pat into a 14- x 10-inch rectangle. Cut into 4 smaller rectangles with a sharp knife. Sprinkle half of each rectangle generously with mozzarella cheese. Top mozzarella with a mound of the spinach mixture, allowing a 3/4-inch margin to the edge. Stretch pizza dough over top of mound and pinch edges to seal, rounding edges at the corners to form half-moon shapes.

Arrange calzones on cookie sheet and bake in the center of oven, 15 minutes or until golden. Cool on a rack, 5 minutes.

Heat sauce in a small pan. Cut calzones in half and serve with marinara sauce, for dipping.

Variation:

For a spinach-artichoke calzone, omit the roasted red peppers and replace with 1 cup coarsely chopped artichoke hearts. Continue with the recipe instructions.

Bean Burritos Grande

MAKES 4 LARGE BURRITOS

1 tablespoon corn or vegetable oil

1 jalapeno or serrano pepper, seeded and
finely chopped

3 cloves garlic, minced

1 small onion, finely chopped and divided into
2 equal portions

1 can (14 ounces) spicy vegetarian refried beans

1 teaspoon ground cumin (1/3 palmful)

A few drops Tabasco brand or other cayenne
pepper sauce

1 can (14 ounces) black beans, drained

2 medium plum tomatoes, seeded and diced

1 ripe avocado, pitted and diced

Juice of 1/2 lemon

Four 12-inch flour tortillas

8 ounces taco sauce

10 ounces shredded Monterey Jack or Pepper
Jack cheese (about 21/2 cups)

A handful fresh cilantro, finely chopped
(optional)

Coarse salt, to taste

Heat a medium skillet over medium heat. Add oil and sauté jalapeno, garlic, and half of the chopped onions, 3 minutes. Add refried beans and stir until beans combine with the onion, garlic, and pepper mixture. Season with cumin and cayenne pepper sauce and stir in black beans. Remove from heat.

In a small bowl, toss tomato and avocado with the lemon juice.

Heat a griddle or large nonstick skillet over medium-high heat. When griddle is hot, sear tortillas 30 to 45 seconds per side and pile them on a work surface.

To assemble, spread a tortilla with a thin layer of taco sauce, leaving a 1-inch border to the edge. Scatter shredded cheese down the center of the tortilla.

Top cheese with a little of the remaining onion, and then add diced tomato, avocado, and a sprinkle of cilantro. Season with a little salt, to taste. Pile a quarter of the bean mixture on top of the veggies and cheese. Tuck top and bottom of the tortilla in, give it a quarter-turn, and roll burrito up and over. Split each burrito in half. Serve with a green salad and extra taco sauce, for dipping.

Quesadillas with Pico de Gallo (Salsa) and Chunky Guacamole

MAKES 4 QUESADILLAS AND 4 SERVINGS EACH, SALSA AND GUACAMOLE

PICO DE GALLO (SALSA):
3 medium plum tomatoes, seeded and diced
1 small jalapeno pepper, seeded and
    finely chopped
1/2 small onion, finely chopped
A few sprigs fresh cilantro, finely chopped
Coarse salt, to taste

GUACAMOLE:
2 medium ripe avocados, pitted and diced
Juice of 1 lemon
1 jalapeno pepper, seeded and finely chopped
1/2 small onion, finely chopped
Coarse salt, to taste

QUESADILLAS:
Corn oil or vegetable oil-based cooking spray
Four 12-inch flour tortillas
10 ounces shredded Monterey Jack, Pepper Jack
    or smoked cheddar cheese (2 cups)

Preheat a large nonstick skillet or griddle pan over medium to medium-high heat.

Combine salsa ingredients in a small bowl and set aside.

Mash avocado with lemon juice into a chunky paste. Stir in jalapeno, onion, and salt, to taste.

Spray griddle or skillet with cooking spray and heat a tortilla, 30 seconds. Flip tortilla. Top one-half of the tortilla with a generous layer of cheese and fold over into a half-moon shape. Grill, 30 to 45 seconds longer on each side, and remove to serving plate. Repeat with remaining tortillas.

To serve, cut each quesadilla into 4 wedges and top with rounded spoonfuls of salsa and guacamole.

Bruschetta with Vegetable and Bean Dips and Spreads

For snacking, combine 1 recipe of bruschetta with your choice of any 1 of the dips or spreads. For a party offering for 8 to 10, mix and match a double batch of toasts with any 2 spreads.

Bruschetta: Garlic Cocktail Toasts
20 TO 24 SLICES

1 loaf crusty, semolina bread, preferably day-old
6 cloves cracked garlic
Extra-virgin olive oil, for drizzling

Cut bread into 1/2-inch slices. Rub the bread with cracked cloves of garlic and toast on both sides under the broiler. Place the "used" garlic cloves in a small dish and cover with olive oil. Microwave on high, 20 to 30 seconds. Lightly brush or drizzle oil across toasted breads. Serve on a platter surrounding a bowl of your favorite dip or spread.

Eggplant Tapenade
MAKES 1 1/2 TO 2 CUPS

1 medium eggplant

2 cloves garlic, cracked

3 tablespoons extra-virgin
   olive oil (a couple of glugs)

A handful fresh flat-leaf parsley (1/4 cup)

Coarse salt and black pepper, to taste

2 or 3 pinches allspice

Preheat oven to 425 degrees F.

Pierce one side of eggplant with the tines of a fork or the tip of a small knife. Place the whole eggplant directly on center oven rack, pierced side-up. Roast eggplant for 20 minutes or until it's tender and a little deflated. Remove and let cool on a plate. When cool enough to handle, peel, using a knife. Transfer the peeled eggplant into a food processor. Add garlic, olive oil, parsley, salt, pepper, and allspice. Pulse the processor until a paste forms. Transfer to a small bowl and serve with bruschetta.

Artichoke Crema

MAKES 1 1/2 CUPS

1 can (14 ounces) quartered artichoke
hearts, drained
2 cloves garlic, crushed
3 tablespoons extra-virgin olive oil
(a couple glugs)
1/2 teaspoon thyme (3 or 4 pinches)
Coarse salt, to taste
Juice of 1/2 lemon

Place artichoke hearts in a food processor.

Cover garlic with olive oil and microwave on high, 1 minute. Allow oil and garlic to cool, 5 minutes and add to food processor. Season with thyme and a few pinches coarse salt. Add lemon juice, pulse grind into a paste, and transfer to a small bowl. Serve with bruschetta toasts.

Spinach Artichoke Dip
MAKES 6 SERVINGS

10 ounces chopped frozen spinach, defrosted
and squeezed dry

1 can (14 ounces) artichoke hearts in
water, drained

2 cloves garlic, cracked and peeled

1 cup reduced-fat mayonnaise

1 cup grated Parmigiano Reggiano or Romano
cheese

8 ounces shredded part-skim mozzarella cheese

1/2 teaspoon ground thyme

1/2 teaspoon nutmeg, ground or freshly grated

Coarse black pepper, to taste

Your choice: cubed crusty bread, pretzel rods
red pepper strips, celery sticks

Preheat oven to 400 degrees F.

Place spinach in a bowl and set aside. Pulse artichoke hearts and garlic in a food processor coarsely. Add artichokes and garlic to spinach. Combine with mayonnaise and grated cheese. Fold in mozzarella and seasonings. Place in a small casserole or oven-safe dish. Bake 15 to 20 minutes 'til golden and bubbly. Serve immediately.

Note: If you are taking this dip to a party, bake it when you arrive; always serve this dip fresh and hot from the oven.

Happy Snacking!

White Bean Dip
MAKES 1 1/2 CUPS

1 can (14 ounces) cannellini beans, rinsed
    and drained
1 clove garlic, cracked from skin
A generous drizzle extra-virgin olive oil
    (1 1/2 tablespoons)
4 sprigs fresh mint leaves (a palmful)
6 sprigs fresh thyme leaves, stripped from stem
    (2 tablespoons)
Coarse salt and black pepper, to taste

Pulse all ingredients in food processor until a smooth paste forms and transfer to a bowl. Serve with bruschetta or flavored chips such as onion and garlic Yukon Gold Chips (Terra).

Tomato and Onion Relish
MAKES 1 $1/2$ CUPS

6 plum tomatoes, seeded and finely chopped
1 small boiling onion, finely chopped
A handful fresh flat-leaf parsley, finely chopped
A generous drizzle extra-virgin olive oil
Coarse salt and black pepper, to taste

Combine all ingredients and serve immediately with the bruschetta.

Red Pepper and Sun-Dried Tomato Spread
MAKES 1 1/2 CUPS

1 jar (14 to 16 ounces) roasted red peppers,
    drained or 2 medium fresh roasted
    red peppers
3 ounces sun-dried tomatoes
1 clove garlic, cracked from skin
A palmful capers, drained (about 2 tablespoons)
A generous drizzle extra-virgin olive oil
    (about 2 tablespoons)
A handful fresh flat-leaf parsley
Coarse salt and freshly ground black pepper,
    to taste

Drain peppers well and place in the bowl of a food processor.

Simmer tomatoes in a small pan of boiling water, 5 minutes or until tender. Drain tomatoes and add to processor. Add garlic, capers, olive oil, and parsley to the peppers and tomatoes. Pulse grind into a paste. Season with salt and pepper, to taste. Serve with garlic toasts or breadsticks.

Wild Mushroom Spread
MAKES 1 1/2 TO 2 CUPS

24 crimini mushrooms (baby portobellos)

12 fresh shiitake mushrooms

2 tablespoons butter

2 tablespoons extra-virgin olive oil (2 turns around the pan)

4 cloves garlic, cracked from skins and crushed

Coarse salt and black pepper, to taste

1/2 cup dry sherry

A handful fresh flat-leaf parsley

Wipe mushrooms with damp paper towels and coarsely chop.

Heat a skillet over medium to medium-high heat. Add butter and oil, then garlic, mushrooms, and salt and pepper, to taste. Cook mushrooms, 10 minutes, until tender and dark. Add sherry and allow liquid to reduce for 1 minute. Remove from heat and transfer to a food processor. Let mushrooms cool 5 to 10 minutes, before adding parsley and pulse grinding into a paste.

Serve with bruschetta.

Olive Tapenade

MAKES 1 CUP

1 cup oil-cured black olives (3 scoops from the
   bulk olive bins)

2 tablespoons extra-virgin olive oil
   (a generous drizzle)

2 cloves garlic, cracked from skins

6 anchovy fillets

3 ounces sun-dried tomatoes (a couple handfuls)

1/2 teaspoon allspice (a few pinches)

Black pepper, to taste

Pit olives by placing the flat of a knife on top of the olive and whacking the blade flat with the heel of your hand.

Place olives in a food processor bowl.

Warm a small skillet over medium heat. Add olive oil and garlic to the hot pan. When garlic speaks by sizzling in oil, add anchovies and sauté until they melt into the olive oil. Remove from heat and set aside to cool.

Simmer sun-dried tomatoes in water 'til tender, about 5 minutes. Drain and coarsely chop.

Add tomatoes to the olives and pour in anchovy oil. Season with a little allspice and black pepper and pulse grind into a paste. Serve with garlic toasts.

Spicy Hummus
MAKES 2 CUPS

1 can (15 ounces) chick peas (garbanzo beans),
  drained
1 large clove garlic, cracked away from skin
3 rounded tablespoons tahini paste (ground
  sesame paste)
Juice of 1 small lemon
1 teaspoon ground cumin (1/3 palmful)
1 teaspoon ground coriander (1/3 palmful)
1/2 teaspoon crushed red pepper flakes
Coarse salt, to taste
Pita bread

Combine all ingredients in a food processor, and pulse grind into a thick spread. Serve with toasted wedges of pita breads. For a more substantial snack, fill a pita pocket with hummus and top with lettuce, tomato, onion, and chopped hot pepper rings.

Pita Pit-zas

Pita Pit-zas are easy snack suppers. If you have kids in the house, making Pita Pit-zas is a fun activity with delicious edible results.

Antipasto Pit-zas
MAKES 4 PITA PIZZAS

4 pita breads (8 inch)
2 large cloves garlic, crushed
2 tablespoons extra-virgin olive oil
1 cup shredded provolone (a couple handfuls)
1 cup shredded mozzarella (a couple handfuls)
1/2 cup each:
    roasted red pepper, diced
    artichoke hearts, chopped
    hot cherry or pepperoncini peppers
    hearts of palm, thinly sliced
    large green and black olives, coarsely
        chopped
2 tablespoons chopped fresh parsley (a handful)
Crushed red pepper flakes
Dried Italian seasoning

Preheat oven to 400 degrees F.

Rub pitas with cracked garlic and brush lightly with olive oil. Toast in oven, 2 to 3 minutes, on cookie sheets. Let cool, 1 minute. Top each round with provolone, mozzarella, roasted pepper, artichoke, hot peppers, hearts of palm, and olives. Sprinkle with parsley, crushed red pepper flakes, and a little dried Italian seasoning. Bake 10 minutes, or until cheese begins to bubble and edges of pizza brown.

Tomato Basil Pit-zas
MAKES 4 PITA PIZZAS

4 pita breads (8 inch)
2 cloves garlic, crushed
Extra-virgin olive oil
1 pound fresh mozzarella or smoked fresh
    mozzarella, thinly sliced
2 vine-ripe tomatoes, seeded and thinly sliced
3 or 4 leaves fresh basil, torn

Preheat oven to 400 degrees F.

Rub pitas with cracked garlic and brush lightly with olive oil. Toast in oven, 2 to 3 minutes, on cookie sheets. Remove from oven, then top with mozzarella and tomatoes. Return to oven and cook, 6 to 8 minutes longer, until mozzarella melts and edges of pizzas brown. Top with torn basil leaves and serve.

Pesto Pit-zas with Spinach and Brocolli
MAKES 4 PITA PIZZAS

4 pita breads (8 inch)
1/2 cup basil pesto, homemade or store bought
1 cup part-skim ricotta cheese
1 cup cooked broccoli florets, chopped
1 package (10 ounces) frozen chopped spinach,
    defrosted and squeezed dry
2 cloves garlic, finely chopped
Salt and pepper, to taste
2 cups shredded mozzarella

Preheat oven to 400 degrees F.

Toast pita bread on cookie sheets, 2 to 3 minutes. Remove from oven and set aside.

Combine pesto, ricotta, broccoli, spinach, and garlic. Season with salt and pepper. Top each pita with 1/4 of the pesto and vegetable mixture, then top with mozzarella. Return pizzas to the oven and bake, 12 minutes, or until cheese bubbles and begins to brown.

Mexican Pit-zas

MAKES 4 PITA PIZZAS

4 pita breads (8 inch)

1 cup vegetarian refried beans (one-half, 15-ounce can)

$1/2$ cup mild taco sauce

2 cups shredded Monterey Jack or Pepper Jack cheese

2 small plum tomatoes, diced

2 scallions, chopped

1 jalapeno pepper, seeded and finely chopped

SUGGESTED GARNISHES:

chopped cilantro

sour cream

guacamole

Preheat oven to 400 degrees F.

Toast pita bread on cookie sheets, 2 to 3 minutes. Remove from oven and let cool, 1 or 2 minutes.

Spread pita breads with a thin layer of refried beans. Top with a few spoonfuls of taco sauce. Sprinkle a generous amount of cheese over each pita, then top with tomatoes, scallions, and jalapeno. Bake 12 minutes, or until cheese is bubbly and begins to brown.

Index